Table of Contents

- 2 — The British Period in Florida, 1763-1783
- 7 — William Bartram Trail
- 8 — Regional Map of Sites
- 10 — Northwest Region
- 16 — North Central Region
- 20 — Northeast Region
- 47 — Central Region
- 57 — South Region
- 62 — Selected Bibliography
- 63 — Acknowledgments

Credits

Author of Introduction, Sidebars, and Bibliography
Dr. Daniel L. Schafer, Professor Emeritus of History, University of North Florida, Jacksonville, Florida

Author of Site Entries and Editor
Frederick P. Gaske, Historic Preservation Consultant, Tallahassee, Florida

Project Administration
Malinda Horton, Florida Association of Museums, Tallahassee, Florida

Graphic Design
Patti Cross, Osprey, Florida

This publication has been financed in part with historic preservation grant assistance provided by the Division of Historical Resources, Florida Department of State, assisted by the Florida Historical Commission. However, the contents and opinions do not necessarily reflect the views and opinions of the Florida Department of State, nor does the mention of trade names or commercial products constitute endorsement or recommendation by the Florida Department of State.

© 2014 Florida Department of State, Division of Historical Resources

The British Period in Florida, 1763-1783

At the end of the Seven Years' War in 1763 (the French and Indian War in North America), and again at the conclusion of the American War of Independence in 1783, representatives of nations at war met in Paris to negotiate treaties that dramatically altered the course of Florida history. In 1763, Great Britain claimed as the victor's reward a vast expanse of overseas territory: Florida was acquired from Spain in a trade for Cuba, and the territory between Spanish Florida and the Mississippi River was gained from France. The City of New Orleans and the Isle of Orleans were omitted, but the British also gained French Canada. Amidst the celebratory atmosphere of postwar Britain, no one could have imagined that 20 years later another round of peace talks would be convened in Paris, and British East and West Florida would be ceded back to Spain.

In 1763, Britain divided its new South Atlantic and Gulf Coast acquisitions into two provinces with a common border on the Apalachicola River – East Florida and West Florida. As the only city in East Florida, St. Augustine became the capital; in West Florida, Pensacola was chosen as the capital over Mobile, Biloxi, and Natchez. British troops took control of St. Augustine in July 1763, and the Union Jack was raised at Pensacola one month later.

The Spanish residents of Florida had been bypassed by fighting during the war, having experienced a rare two decades without a rebellion or an invasion. However, they suffered devastating personal losses of homes and properties as a result of the 1763 Treaty of Paris. Only three Spanish families in East Florida chose to remain under the British Flag; the other 3,500 residents were transported from St. Augustine to Havana and Veracruz, Mexico. In British West Florida, 800 Spanish subjects were transported from Pensacola, leaving approximately 700 French settlers near Mobile, and approximately 28,000 Choctaw, Chickasaw, Creek and other Native Americans in villages west of Pensacola, closer to the Mississippi River.

The first governors of the new British colonies, James Grant in East Florida and George Johnstone in West Florida, arrived at their respective capital cities late in 1764 intent on recruiting settlers and promoting agricultural development. With only a few companies of British soldiers, three holdover Spanish families, and small villages of Creek migrants recently settled on vacant land, East Florida was an empty province.

A map of East and West Florida, ca. 1765.
(Image courtesy of the Special Collections Department, University of South Florida)

Like its neighbor to the east, West Florida was desperately in need of settlers. Both governors realized, however, that their first priority had to be negotiating land concessions and peace treaties with the Native Americans residing in their provinces. Both men met those challenges at a series of congresses arranged in 1765 and in subsequent years. Migration could then proceed and farms and plantations could be established without the threat of attacks by hostile natives.

A finely-carved British colonial powder horn, ca. 1765, with the City of St. Augustine on one side (showing) and a meeting between the British and Indians, believed to be the Treaty Picolata conference, on the other.
(Image courtesy of the Museum of Florida History)

The British Period in Florida, 1763-1783

Governor Grant tirelessly promoted plantation development in his province. He encouraged entrepreneurs from England and other British colonies, such as the Carolinas and Georgia, to take advantage of generous land grant policies which would enable them to acquire large tracts in East Florida at little or no cost. In West Florida, Governor Johnstone also promoted immigration and plantation development, but he focused his recruiting efforts on French, German, and Swiss farmers. He also attempted to coax residents of New Orleans to cross the border and settle in West Florida.

Population numbers in both provinces climbed slowly in the early years. By the early 1770s dozens of farms and plantations had been established in East Florida along the major inland rivers and along the Atlantic coast for approximately 90 miles south of St. Augustine. At today's Ormond Beach, the Scot merchant Richard Oswald sent agents, overseers, and 240 enslaved Africans to a 20,000-acre estate. At two 20,000-acre tracts at Mosquito Inlet known as Smyrnea Plantation, Dr. Andrew Turnbull was the resident manager and partner of two absentee owners, Sir William Duncan, royal physician to King George III, and George Grenville, a former prime minister. Turnbull traveled to the Mediterranean in 1767-1768 to

Native Americans in British Florida

The native population of Florida has been estimated by scholars to have numbered approximately 350,000 persons prior to the arrival of Europeans. The population was drastically reduced after European explorers and colonizers introduced diseases for which Florida natives had no immunities, and slaving raids and warfare eliminated nearly all of the remaining original Native Americans.

Beginning in the 1720s, encouraged by the Spanish, small numbers of Native Americans began moving south from Georgia to settle on vacant lands in Florida where earlier villages had once been located. These Creek migrants were attracted to the empty land and bountiful hunting grounds that supplied them with the skins and furs they traded to Spanish merchants.

The Native Americans present in East Florida when the British arrived in 1763 were still following Creek cultural traditions, yet they were in a transformative process that would result in their becoming an independent people known as the Seminole. The small settlements grew in numbers during the British years, and by 1774 nine substantial villages were located on the Suwannee near the Gulf Coast, at Palatka on the St. Johns, and near today's Brooksville, Tallahassee, and Gainesville. In West Florida the Choctaw, Chickasaw, Creek, and smaller groups totaled approximately 28,000 people, but they were primarily settled closer to the Mississippi River, and most resided beyond the border of today's state of Florida.

In both provinces, congresses held between 1765 and 1775 resulted in generally peaceful relations. Land concessions granted by the Indians permitted British population growth and agricultural development, and in return the Indians were promised unlimited access to hunting grounds and strict regulation of unlawful practices by the British deerskin traders. Creek and Seminole hunters were assured they could continue their lucrative sales of skins and furs. The leading British trading company was operated by James Spalding and Roger Kelsall, headquartered at St. Simon's Island in Georgia, but with two stores located west of the St. Johns River. The Spalding Upper Store was located at today's Astor, and the Lower Trade Store was located at Stoke's Landing, south of present-day Palatka.

Creek and Seminole were frequently seen in the streets and stores in St. Augustine, selling horses and cattle and purchasing goods at the town market to carry to their temporary camps outside the town walls. Seminole men crossed fields at farms in the province while on their annual hunts, and they often sold or bartered fresh meat to families at the settlements. By promoting peaceful policies rather than aggressive military expansion, loyal East Florida gained an important ally during the American War for Independence. Creek and Seminole warriors fought as allies of the East Florida Rangers against invaders from Georgia.

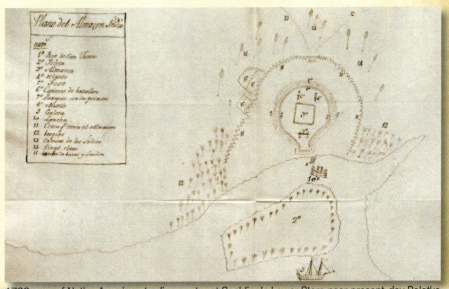

1792 map of Native American trading center at Spalding's Lower Store near present-day Palatka.
(Image courtesy of the Library of Congress)

The British Period in Florida, 1763-1783

African Americans in Florida's British Years

Governor James Grant, following the example of South Carolina, aspired to transform East Florida into a thriving colony with exports of agricultural staples cultivated by enslaved Africans. He warned that white laborers became lazy or debilitated by the heat and abandoned rural settlements for the colonial towns. Employing white artisans was expensive, Grant reasoned, and planters were advised to train slaves to be skilled tradesmen: "this country can only be brought to [a] rich and plentiful state by the labor of slaves."

With the exception of Dr. Andrew Turnbull's Smyrnea Plantation, worked by 1,400 indentured laborers from Italy, Greece and Minorca, East Florida's rural labor force was overwhelmingly black and enslaved. Planters purchased slaves born in New World colonies and "seasoned" Africans who had resided in the colony long enough to be familiar with the crops and language. Eventually, less expensive "New Negroes" imported direct from Africa were added.

The enslaved blacks, men and women alike, were primarily field laborers, but plantations also had slave carpenters, wagon makers, wheelwrights, brick and stone masons, coopers, domestic servants, cooks, seamstresses, weavers, dairymaids, basket makers, gardeners, drovers, cattle keepers, hunters, fishermen, sawyers, naval stores manufacturers, even overseers and plantation managers. Slaves in St. Augustine were domestics, stevedores, sailors, and artisans.

Slaves transformed wetlands into rice fields with drains, dams, and fresh water lakes, others were indigo and sugar makers, some worked for wages in St. Augustine, still others joined companies of the East Florida militia, the St. Johns Rangers. During the American Revolution, one plantation manager organized a patrol of twelve armed slave men.

Treatment of slaves varied by owner, overseer, weather, available food supply, and labor conditions. Conditions in St. Augustine were generally better for slaves than on plantations. Plantations were generally self-sufficient in provisions, but extreme weather conditions caused shortages and hungry times. Records of physical treatment are scarce but documents of floggings exist, even an account of a death caused by a flogging, an incident dismissed as an "unlucky accident." Slaves escaped to the forests and swamps; others were sheltered in Native American villages. To minimize rebelliousness, owners tried to equalize gender numbers, but a heavy male imbalance led to numerous problems.

Some owners treated slaves humanely, including Governor Grant whose domestic staff of ten included Baptiste, who was trained as a chef in Paris and traveled with Grant until his death and burial at the Grant family cemetery in Scotland. A few slaves self-purchased freedom; others were freed at the death of their owner. One freed slave purchased his wife's freedom on a monthly installment plan. While rare, the possibility of independence from their owners was possible.

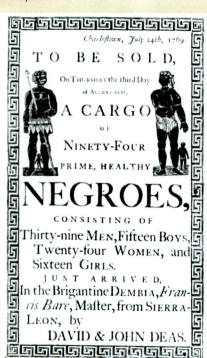

Advertisement for slave sale at Charleston, South Carolina, 1769.
(Image courtesy of the Virginia Foundation for the Humanities and the University of Virginia)

recruit 1,400 indentured laborers from Greece, Italy, and Minorca.

The main product exported from East Florida was indigo dye, grown and processed at most estates in the province. Many of the planters cultivated rice and cotton and most were self-sufficient in production of provisions. Promising experiments with sugar cultivation were underway by the early 1770s. The outbreak of the War of American Independence in 1775, however, meant that ships carrying indigo to markets in Britain were subject to attack and confiscation by privateers and Patriot warships. But war also terminated sales of forest products from New England and Carolina to the Royal Navy and Britain's Caribbean colonies, creating a market that Florida planters were able to supply. Laborers were transferred from indigo fields to what appeared in the 1770s to be unlimited stands of pine, cypress, and live oak timber. Enslaved Africans cut trees, squared timber, and harvested turpentine, pitch and tar to supply British needs.

In West Florida the land around Pensacola was sandy and infertile, but along the Amite and Mississippi Rivers to the west some of the richest farm land in North America was idle until late in the British years. Adventurers were slow to recognize this opportunity and consequently exports of deerskins and furs continued to be the mainstay of the West Florida economy. Another factor that hindered the growth of settlements was the 1768 order from the War Office in London to withdraw garrisons from Manchac and Natchez. By the early 1770s news of the abundant fertile soil along the western rivers spread to Britain's other North American

The British Period in Florida, 1763-1783

colonies, prompting a rush of emigrants to West Florida. By the time they selected tracts and initiated settlements, however, the American War of Independence was underway and further population growth and development ceased. Given more time and peaceful conditions, British West Florida would have become a prosperous colony.

With the exception of a 1778 plundering raid downriver by James Willing, a former West Florida resident, the province's towns and settlements were spared from fighting in the early years of the American Revolution. The stable leadership of Peter Chester, the fifth person to fill the governor's seat, was partly responsible, but the presence of John Stuart in Pensacola by 1776 was an important factor. Stuart, superintendent of Indian affairs in the Southern Department from 1762 to 1779, organized a militia of mounted rangers, and in May 1778 negotiated an alliance with the Creek Indians. The War Office helped by restoring the garrisons at Manchac and Natchez and building a new fort at Baton Rouge.

Soon after these changes took effect, Spain declared war on Britain in June 1779. Bernardo de Gálvez, governor of Spanish Louisiana, led an army that captured Manchac, Baton Rouge and Natchez by September 1779, and Fort Charlotte at Mobile the following March. A hurricane prevented Gálvez from attacking Fort George and Pensacola until March 1781. Two months later the British garrison surrendered, and West Florida again became a Spanish possession.

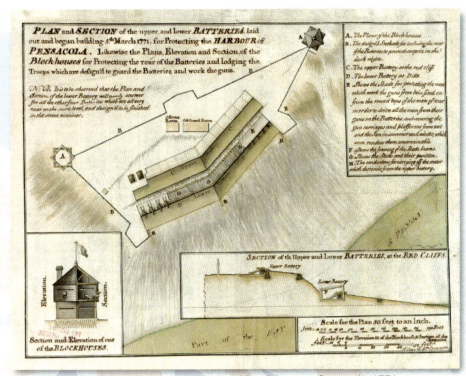

Plan of British fortifications at present-day site of Fort Barrancas, Pensacola, 1771.
(Image courtesy of the George A. Smathers Libraries, University of Florida)

East Florida, though subject to numerous cross-border plundering raids that destroyed settlements between the St. Marys and St. Johns rivers and invasions from Georgia that were blocked by British defenders, remained loyal to Britain. During the latter stages of the Revolution, British strength in East Florida increased as supporters of King George III fled from Georgia and South Carolina to the protection of loyal forces. Large numbers of troop reinforcements arrived at St. Augustine in the summer of 1778 to prepare for an invasion of Georgia and South Carolina. The artisans, dock workers, and sailors on shore leave who accompanied the troops, along with hundreds of Loyalist refugees, created unprecedented opportunities for local farmers and businessmen.

Meanwhile, the war was going badly for Britain. The loss of West Florida to Bernardo de Gálvez in May 1781 was followed in October by the surrender in Virginia of Lord Charles

English pattern infantry saber, ca. 1742-1760.
(Image courtesy of the Museum of Florida History)

The British Period in Florida, 1763-1783

Artist rendering of the British sloop *Industry*, which wrecked on a sandbar off St. Augustine in 1764 while carrying supplies for the British army garrison at the city.
(Image courtesy of the St. Augustine Lighthouse and Museum)

Cornwallis and his 8,000-man army to General George Washington. British delegates sent to Paris began negotiating peace terms and the war in North America was ended. It was eventually decided that East Florida would become a sanctuary for Loyalists from other British provinces. Thousands of refugees were transported from Savannah and Charleston to St. Augustine and provided emergency rations, tools and seeds to plant provisions at unoccupied rural tracts. By the end of December 1782, more than 6,000 refugees had arrived in East Florida, and eventually the population increased to between 17,000 and 18,000 residents. Governor Patrick Tonyn was elated by the rapid population increase, and predicted it would result in a "happy era for this province." He was convinced that the new settlers regarded East Florida as a "safe asylum and permanent residence" and praised their participation in the surging economy based on exports of timber and naval stores to Britain's Caribbean colonies.

Tonyn's hopes for a "happy era" were ended in January 1783, when he received news that peace negotiators in Paris had agreed to end the War of American Independence. Twenty years after one war had ended with Spanish Florida ceded to Great Britain, representatives of the United States of America met with negotiators from Britain at the Paris hotel rooms of Richard Oswald, the London merchant and absentee owner of Mount Oswald Plantation in East Florida. Terms of the 1783 Treaty of Paris granted sovereignty of East and West Florida to Spain.

Lieutenant Governor John Moultrie was devastated by the news. Concerning the thousands of loyal subjects who had only recently built settlements in East Florida and were now abandoned by Britain, Moultrie lamented: "What shall become of these poor unfortunate but virtuous people I cannot divine." Moultrie himself felt betrayed, charging that he and his family had been "turned adrift" to "again seek a resting place."

The formal change of flags took place at the Plaza in St. Augustine on July 12, 1784. Spanish Governor Vizente Manuel de Zéspedes took charge of the government buildings and Fort St. Mark, restoring its former name, the Castillo de San Marcos.

British governor Tonyn was among the last to leave East Florida, after remaining in the province to supervise the departure of thousands of disillusioned Loyalists. On November 10, 1785, Tonyn boarded a troop transport bound for England, symbolizing the end of British rule in Florida. The flag of Spain would fly above the Castillo de San Marcos for the next 36 years, when it would be replaced in 1821 by the Stars and Stripes of the United States of America.

Ship's bell from the "Storm Wreck," a British ship that wrecked off St. Augustine while carrying Loyalist refugees there from Charleston, South Carolina in 1782.
(Image courtesy of the St. Augustine Lighthouse and Museum)

William Bartram Trail

"William Bartram Trail" Historical Markers

The American-born naturalist William Bartram (1739 – 1823) first came to East Florida in 1765 with his father, John Bartram, the King's Botanist for North America, on a botanical collecting expedition. After his father returned to Philadelphia in 1766, William Bartram stayed in East Florida to establish a plantation on a 500-acre land grant along the St. Johns River northwest of St. Augustine. His attempts to produce crops such as indigo were not successful and he abandoned the enterprise within the year. He stayed in Florida to work as a surveyor, survived a shipwreck near New Smyrna, and, in 1767, he returned to Philadelphia.

In 1773, William Bartram embarked upon an epic four year journey through the southern British colonies, which now constitute eight states. He made numerous drawings of the flora and fauna he observed during his travels, and kept extensive notes on the native plants, animals, Indians, settlers, and settlements he encountered. Among the colonies he visited, Bartram traveled extensively through East Florida and made a short visit to West Florida. In 1791, he published his findings in *Travels through North and South Carolina, Georgia, East and West Florida, the Cherokee Country, etc.* It became an immediate success not only in America but in Europe as well, where it was published in six different languages. The book is not only significant for its scientific observations, but also as an important historical source for the British colonial period and the American Indian.

In 1976, the Bartram Trail Conference, Inc. was established to locate and memorialize the route of Bartram's travels through the Southeast. Included in its activities is the erection of historical markers in cooperation with national organizations, state agencies and local groups, which mark Bartram's route of travel. In Florida, at least 20 such historical markers for the "William Bartram Trail Traced 1773-1777" have been erected, all topped with the logo of the National Council of State Garden Clubs or its successor the National Garden Clubs Inc. Each marker contains a short summary of Bartram's activities in that area, and lists local marker sponsors.

The markers are located in the following counties: Alachua (Kanapaha Botanical Garden, Paynes Prairie, and Newberry), Brevard (two in Canaveral National Seashore), Escambia (two in Pensacola and one at the Florida/Alabama state line), Indian River (Sebastian), Marion (Salt Springs), Nassau (Fernandina Beach), Orange (Winter Park), Putnam (Palatka and East Palatka), Seminole (I-4 rest area near Longwood), St. Johns (Picolata, St. Augustine Beach, and Switzerland), and Volusia (Hontoon Island State Park and Volusia).

Stokes Landing kiosk panels, Putnam County Bartram Trail.
(Images courtesy of Sam Carr, Bartram Trail in Putnam County Committee)

Northwest Region
(Pages 10-15)

ESCAMBIA COUNTY
- Colonial Archaeological Trail
- Fort George Park
- Naval Air Station Pensacola
- T.T. Wentworth, Jr. Florida State Museum

FRANKLIN COUNTY
- Fort Gadsden

North Central Region
(Pages 16-19)

ALACHUA COUNTY
- P.K. Yonge Library of Florida History, University of Florida
- William Bartram State Historical Marker

DIXIE COUNTY
- Jackson Water Hole Park
- Oldtown State Historical Marker

LEON COUNTY
- Goodwood Museum and Gardens
- Museum of Florida History
- State Library of Florida/ State Archives of Florida

WAKULLA COUNTY
- Fort St. Marks, San Marcos de Apalache Historic State Park

Northeast Region
(Pages 20-46)

CLAY COUNTY
- Fort San Fransisco de Pupo State Historical Marker

DUVAL COUNTY
- Delius House
- Historic King's Road Historical Marker
- King's Road Monument
- Museum of Science and History
- Site of Cow Ford State Historical Marker
- Mandarin Museum and Historical Society

FLAGLER COUNTY
- King's Road State Historical Marker

NASSAU COUNTY
- Battle of Thomas Creek State Historical Marker
- Battle of Alligator Creek Bridge Historical Marker
- Revolutionary War Invasion of British East Florida Historical Marker

PUTNAM COUNTY
- Putnam County Bartram Trail
- Rollestown State Historical Marker

ST. JOHNS COUNTY
- Fort San Diego State Historical Marker
- Picolata State Historical Marker
- Governor Grant's Plantations State Historical Marker
- Avero House
- De Mesa-Sanchez House
- Evergreen Cemetery
- Father Miguel O'Reilly House Museum
- Fort St. Mark, Castillo de San Marcos National Monument
- Fort Matanzas National Monument
- Fort Mose Historic State Park
- Government House
- Horruytiner-Lindsley House
- King's Road State Historical Marker
- Oglethorpe Battery Park
- Oldest House Museum Complex
- Pena-Peck House
- Prisoners Of War in St. Augustine During the American Revolution Historical Marker
- St. Augustine Art Association
- St. Augustine Historical Society Research Library
- St. Augustine Lighthouse and Museum
- St. Francis Barracks and The King's Bakery
- Tolomato Cemetery
- Tovar House
- Double Bridges and the Old King's Road State Historical Marker
- New Switzerland Plantation Historical Marker
- William Bartram's Plantation State Historical Marker
- William Bartram Scenic and Historic Highway

Pensacola

Central Region
(Pages 47-56)

BREVARD COUNTY
- The Florida Historical Society
- Last Naval Battle of the American Revolutionary War State Historical Marker

LAKE COUNTY
- Holy Trinity Episcopal Church

ORANGE COUNTY
- The English Colony Historical Marker
- Bumby Building
- Rogers Building

OSCEOLA COUNTY
- Narcoossee Schoolhouse
- Former Church of St. Luke and St. Peter

POLK COUNTY
- Acton Community State Historical Marker
- Lodwick School of Aeronautics Historical Marker

VOLUSIA COUNTY
- The Old King's Road Historical Marker
- Dr. Andrew Turnbull Monument
- New Smyrna Museum of History
- Old Fort Park
- Old Stone Wharf
- Turnbull Canal Monument
- Old King's Road State Historical Marker
- Old King's Road Historical Marker
- Tomoka State Park
- Three Chimneys

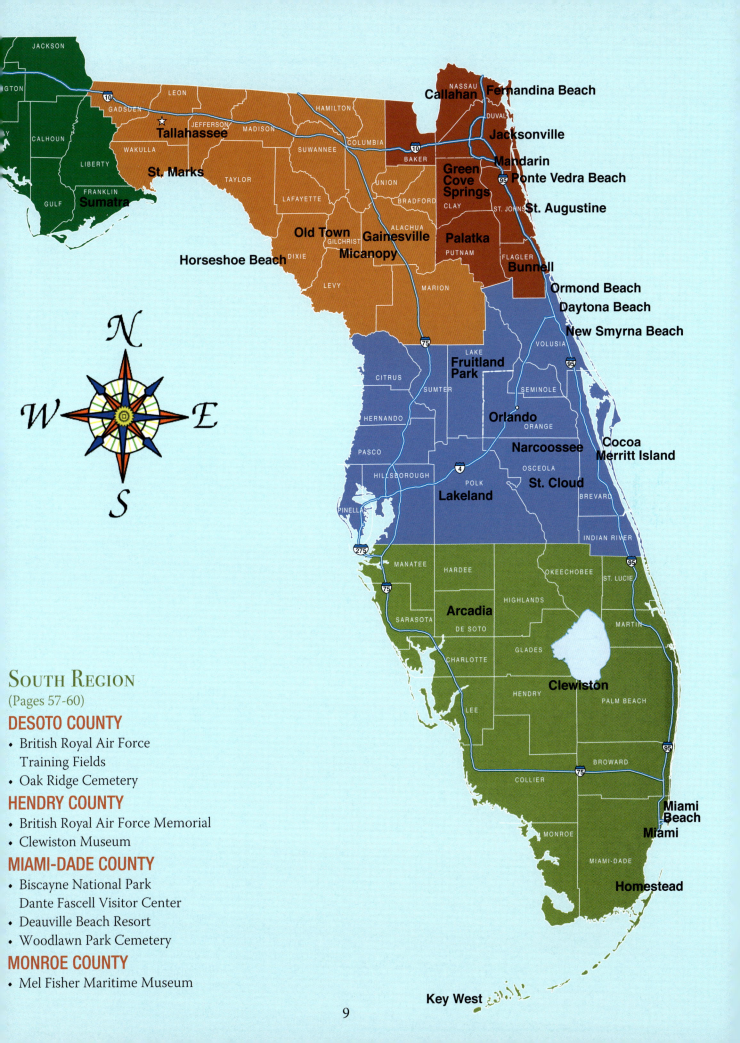

NORTHWEST REGION

ESCAMBIA COUNTY
Pensacola

COLONIAL ARCHAEOLOGICAL TRAIL

Downtown Pensacola
850.474.3015
uwf.edu/anthropology/research/colonial/trail

Stretching from Plaza Ferdinand VII to Seville Square in downtown Pensacola, the Colonial Archaeological Trail covers the area where the British Fort of Pensacola once stood. After Florida was acquired in 1763, the British began to build their own fort to replace the earlier, dilapidated Spanish fort. The old fort was enlarged, expanded, and made more defensible with the addition of four bastions armed with cannons and a dry moat. Parade grounds outside the west wall (present-day Plaza Ferdinand) and east wall (present-day Seville Square) also provided a clear range of fire for defense. By 1778, the wooden stockade fort contained within its walls the commanding officer's house, officers quarters, barracks, other military support buildings, public buildings, and artillery batteries facing Pensacola Bay. Most of the town's houses were located outside of the stockade walls. The fort was surrendered to the Spanish in 1781, along with the rest of the town and other fortifications, after the two-month Battle of Pensacola. None of the British buildings survived to the present day.

The Colonial Archaeological Trail is a self-guided walking tour of excavated ruins of several of the fort buildings with interpretive panels and, at several sites, wooden walkway overlooks. Among the sites on the Trail are the remains of an officers' room/kitchen building constructed by the British shortly after 1775, the commanding officers' compound which was expanded or rebuilt by the British after 1767, and a well most likely constructed for the British soldiers in the fort around 1771. Other Trail sites include the British Government House built in the 1770s which was originally intended as the residence of the Royal Governor and a British garrison kitchen building constructed around 1771.

Map of Pensacola by British surveyor Joseph Purcell, 1778.
(Image courtesy of the Library of Congress)

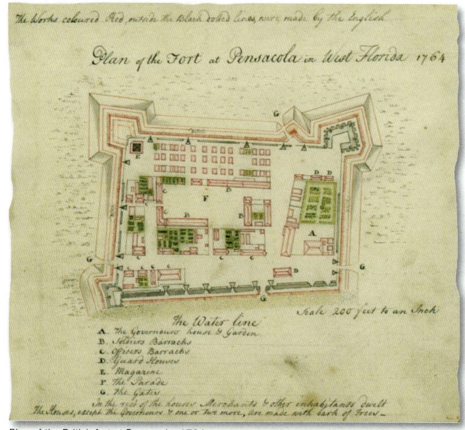
Plan of the British fort at Pensacola, 1764.
(Image courtesy of the Brown University Library)

Northwest Region

Fort George Park

North Palafox Street and West La Rua Street

This small park of approximately one-half acre in the North Hill District of Pensacola contains a reconstruction of a section of Fort George, a British fortification, on its original foundation. In order to protect Pensacola from attack from the north, the British erected an earthen rampart fort surrounded by a dry moat in 1778-1779. Located about 1,000 yards north of the town on Gage Hill, it was named Fort George in honor of the King of England. Along the higher ridge to the northwest of Fort George, the British erected two smaller fortifications of timber and earth, the Queen's Redoubt and the Prince of Wales Redoubt. With Spain's entrance into the war against Great Britain in 1779 during the American Revolution, these fortifications would soon be put to the test. In March 1781, the Spanish Governor of Louisiana, General Bernardo de Gálvez, began an attack on Pensacola after achieving victories against the British at Baton Rouge, Louisiana in 1779 and Mobile, Alabama in 1780. For two months, Gálvez laid siege to Pensacola with a force of Spanish regulars, Spanish colonial

Bernardo de Gálvez and the Spanish Capture of West Florida

For West Florida, the American Revolution occurred at the time the province was experiencing its first significant influx of settlers. Some of the richest farmland in North America, huge unoccupied tracts along the Mississippi River in the vicinity of Natchez and Vicksburg, had beckoned to immigrants for more than a decade, yet few settlers had arrived before the war broke out. The province was spared the violence experienced in other areas until February 1778, when Patriot naval captain James Willing, with fewer than one hundred men, pillaged the Natchez district and continued downriver to Spanish New Orleans to dispose of plunder gathered along the way.

Britain responded by sending troops to forts abandoned years before at Natchez and Manchac and building a new fort at Baton Rouge.

A company of mounted rangers and an infantry regiment formed from within the province provided a temporary sense of security and stabilized the economy, but that ended in June 1779 when Spain joined the war against Britain.

Bernardo de Gálvez, the governor of Spanish Louisiana, assumed command of Spanish forces and focused his first military campaign against the tiny trade center of Manchac, at the junction of the Mississippi River and the Iberville Bayou. Gálvez's army of 1,000 captured Manchac, Baton Rouge, and Natchez by September 1779. Fort Charlotte at Mobile fell to the Spanish army in March 1780, and after a two-month siege of Fort George and Pensacola, Major General John Campbell and Governor Peter Chester surrendered to Gálvez on May 10, 1781. With the surrender of Pensacola, West Florida was once again part of the Spanish colonial empire.

Bernardo de Gálvez, Governor of Spanish Louisiana.
(Image courtesy of the St. Augustine Lighthouse and Museum)

Fort George Park, Pensacola.
(Image courtesy of William Lees, Florida Public Archaeology Network)

British buttons from Fort George, Pensacola, including one from the 16th Regiment of Foot (right).
(Image courtesy of the Florida Division of Historical Resources)

Northwest Region

militia, and allied French soldiers which eventually totaled about 7,000 men. The British defenders consisted of some 2,500 British regulars, German mercenaries, Loyalist provincials, and Indian allies, mostly Creeks and Choctaws. The British held out until May 1781 when a Spanish howitzer shell hit the powder magazine in the Queen's Redoubt killing most of its British defenders. Spanish troops stormed and captured the Redoubt, and then began shelling the remaining British fortifications from their newly captured vantage point. Realizing that his defensive positions were no longer tenable, the British commander, General John Campbell, surrendered Fort George and the town of Pensacola.

Renamed Fort San Miguel by the Spanish, the fort fell into disrepair during the Spanish Second Period and early American Period as fortifications along Pensacola Bay received priority. During the Civil War, Union forces erected an earthen fortification named Fort McClellan in the vicinity of Fort George. Following the war, residential development of

The Battle of Pensacola, 1781.
(Image courtesy of the Library of Congress)

North Hill destroyed most of the remains of Fort George. A small undeveloped section of the fort's remains was purchased by the City of Pensacola in 1974 for use as an interpretive park. Following investigations by State of Florida archaeologists, the City erected a reconstruction of a portion of the fort including ramparts with two 18th century British cannons. Interpretive panels at the park provide information on the fort's history. In May 1981, in commemoration of the 200th anniversary of the Siege of Pensacola, a monument with a bust of General Bernardo de Gálvez at its top was placed in the park by the Gálvez Bicentennial Commission. The monument was damaged in 2012 by vandals who knocked off the bust, but it has since been replaced. In 1996, the Florida Society of the Sons of the American Revolution installed a plaque on a park wall in honor of the 25 American volunteers who served under General Gálvez in the Battle of Pensacola. Two historical markers are also located near the park, one for "Fort George" erected by the Knights of Columbus and a second erected in 1997 by the Florida State Society of the Daughters of the American Revolution to commemorate the "Battle of Pensacola March 9 to May 8, 1781."

British wine bottle from Fort George, Pensacola.
(Image courtesy of the Florida Division of Historical Resources)

Bernardo de Gálvez monument, Fort George Park, Pensacola.
(Image courtesy of William Lees, Florida Public Archaeology Network)

Northwest Region

British Pensacola and West Florida's Governors

British West Florida was bounded on the east by the Apalachicola River and on the west by the Mississippi River. The southern border was fixed at the Gulf of Mexico and Lake Pontchartrain, extending north to the confluence of the Yazoo and Mississippi Rivers. It was a huge and sparsely settled territory covering parts of today's panhandle region of Florida, Alabama, Mississippi, and Louisiana. British soldiers arriving in 1763 found only four small settlements in the province: the old Spanish port of Pensacola on Pensacola Bay, the former French settlements of Mobile and Biloxi on the Gulf, and Natchez on the Mississippi.

Pensacola, the provincial capital, was located on an excellent harbor, but the soil was sandy and infertile. British soldiers were disappointed by the dilapidated fort they found in 1763, and by the 100 bark and palmetto huts without windows or fireplaces that served as troop barracks. Tormented by mosquitoes, the soldiers suffered a high death rate from tropical diseases. The situation had changed little by October 1764, when Governor George Johnstone arrived and found only 112 "poor despicable huts." Fish was a ready food source, but gardens in the sandy soil were infrequent and cattle supplies had to be driven from Mobile.

Elias Durnford, the surveyor general, drew up a new plan for Pensacola in February 1765 that is the basis for the central city of today. Building lots were distributed by lottery and the settlers who came to the town in the next two years built, according to Governor Johnstone, 113 "good buildings." When clay deposits were discovered nearby, brick buildings were constructed.

George Johnstone was the first of five men to serve as governor. Johnstone was a minor naval officer with no administrative experience prior to his patronage appointment, yet his early months in West Florida were energetic and impressive. He held congresses with the Native Americans of the region whose warriors outnumbered the British soldiers so dramatically that in case of war it was clear that Johnstone's side would lose. He also promoted immigration and established an elective colonial assembly, something that would not happen in East Florida until 1781.

Johnstone's flaws, however, were many. His verbose and outlandish quarrels with British army officers and his own cabinet members were alarming, but it was his aggressive demands for a war against the Creek that led to his dismissal in 1767.

Following Johnstone's ouster, Lieutenant Governor Montfort Browne served as interim governor. Browne, possibly more controversial and provocative than Johnstone, held the interim position for more than two years until British West Florida's second governor, John Eliot, arrived in Pensacola. Eliot, a 24-year-old captain in the Royal Navy, was appointed governor in March 1767, but did not arrive

George Johnstone, Governor of West Florida.
(Image courtesy of the Museum of Florida History)

in Pensacola until April 1769. Less than one month later, possibly suffering from a brain tumor, Eliot hanged himself. Montfort Browne again served as interim governor until his participation in a duel led to his departure from the province in February 1770.

Elias Durnford next served as interim until Peter Chester became the third official governor in August 1770. Chester served admirably until 1781, his tenure distinguished by efforts to promote immigration and agriculture in the rich agricultural lands in the Vicksburg and Natchez area along the east bank of the Mississippi River. In May 1781, Governor Chester surrendered the besieged city of Pensacola to a Spanish army under Bernardo de Gálvez, which marked the end of the colony of British West Florida.

RAF monument, Naval Air Station, Pensacola.
Image courtesy of William Lees, Florida Public Archaeology Network

Naval Air Station Pensacola
190 Radford Boulevard
850.452.0111
cnic.navy.mil/regions/cnrse/installations/nas_pensacola.html

NAS Pensacola is often referred to as the "Cradle of Naval Aviation" and the "Annapolis of the Air" in recognition of its role in the history of naval aviation. In 1914, the US Navy established a Naval Aeronautic Station at the site of the closed Pensacola Navy Yard, which in 1917 was renamed the Naval Air Station (NAS). During World War II, over 28,000 naval aviators were trained at NAS Pensacola, including some 4,000 from Great Britain and the British Commonwealth. In their honor, the Royal Air Force (RAF) dedicated an approximately four-foot high granite tablet monument in 1991 at NAS Pensacola in front of Building 624, where the British and Commonwealth pilots lived during their training. Ten British aviators, six from the Royal Navy and four from the Royal Air Force, who died while in training at the Naval Air Station during World War II, are buried in Barrancas National Cemetery at NAS Pensacola.

Northwest Region

T.T. Wentworth, Jr. Florida State Museum

330 South Jefferson Street
850.595.5990
historicpensacola.org

Located in the restored 1907 Old City Hall building, the Wentworth Museum contains three floors of exhibits and interactive displays relating to the history of Pensacola and northwest Florida. The "Struggle for Empire – Spanish, French, and British in Pensacola" gallery on the first floor contains several exhibits on the British Period with related artifacts, including many British items recovered from archaeological excavations in Pensacola.

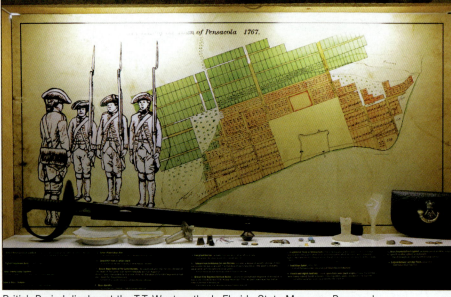
British Period display at the T.T. Wentworth, Jr. Florida State Museum, Pensacola.
(Image courtesy of William Lees, Florida Public Archaeology Network)

View of Pensacola, 1771.
(Image courtesy of the Library of Congress)

British "Brown Bess" musket bayonet from "Negro Fort" (later Fort Gadsden).
(Image courtesy of the Florida Division of Historical Resources)

British trade gun barrel section from "Negro Fort" (later Fort Gadsden).
(Image courtesy of the Florida Division of Historical Resources)

FRANKLIN COUNTY

Sumatra

Fort Gadsden

Apalachicola National Forest
Forest Road 129-B
850.643.2282
fs.usda.gov/apalachicola

Spain's control of Florida during the Second Spanish Period was tenuous at best. Weakened by Napoleon's conquest of Spain and widespread rebellion in her Latin American colonies, the government of Spain's Florida colony was unable to stop British incursions in the colony during the War of 1812. British troops established military outposts in Florida to recruit fugitive American slaves and Indian warriors for their war against the United States without opposition from the Spanish authorities. In the summer of 1814, British troops landed at St. George Island and then erected a fortification on the east bank of the Apalachicola River about 20 miles north of the river's mouth at Prospect Bluff, known as the British Post. In August 1814, some 200 British Royal Marines commanded by Colonel Edward

Northwest Region

Nicolls and Captain George Woodbine landed at Pensacola, but were driven out two months later by American troops commanded by General Andrew Jackson. Nicolls and Woodbine then proceeded to the British Post at Prospect Bluff, which also became referred to as Nicolls' Fort. At this site, the British raised and trained units of escaped slaves known as the Corps of Colonial Marines, and supplied their Indian allies with arms and ammunition. A second, smaller fortification, known as Nicolls' Outpost, was erected upriver at present-day Chattahoochee.

After the war ended, the British evacuated the area in the spring of 1815, but left the well-armed fort with its artillery and munitions in the control of some 300 blacks, many of them fugitive slaves, and their Indian allies. Viewed with alarm by the Americans as a haven for runaway slaves, General Andrew Jackson instructed a force under the command of Colonel Duncan Clinch to attack what the Americans now referred to as the "Negro Fort" in the summer of 1816. On July 27, 1816, following a series of skirmishes at the fort which still flew the British flag, a "hot shot" fired from an American gunboat blew up the fort's powder magazine, destroying the fort and killing all but 30 of its over 300 defenders. The few survivors were taken prisoner. In 1818, General Jackson directed Lieutenant James Gadsden to construct what became known as Fort Gadsden at the site. The fort was occupied by Confederate troops during the Civil War, and afterwards abandoned. The Fort Gadsden site contains interpretive information in a kiosk building and on markers, including a State Historical Marker.

Colonel Edward Nicolls and British Intrigue on the Apalachicola River

During the War of 1812, British Colonel Edward Nicolls and Captain George Woodbine of the Royal Marines sought allies among the Red Stick Creek for a Gulf Coast campaign against the United States. In March 1814 at Horseshoe Bend on the Tallapoosa River in Alabama, the Upper Creek, including the militant faction known as the Red Sticks, were defeated by an army led by American General Andrew Jackson. Many of the Red Stick warriors fled with their families to Spanish Florida and established settlements along the Apalachicola River. Nicolls and Woodbine visited these camps to recruit soldiers for the Black British Colonial Marines. They also recruited Seminole and Black Seminole from Florida and encouraged enslaved blacks from Georgia to desert their masters and join the British army.

The recruits were armed and trained by Captain Woodbine to join with British forces in an attack on New Orleans. A fort was constructed 20 miles upriver on the Apalachicola River at Prospect Bluff and fortified with an arsenal of weapons. Nicolls disregarded the fact that the fort was located within the sovereign boundary of Spanish Florida.

After the resounding American victory by Andrew Jackson's army at the Battle of New Orleans in January of 1815, Nicolls withdrew British troops and 400 Black Colonial Marines from Prospect Bluff to new quarters at Tampa Bay and Manatee River (today's Bradenton), where black and Native American villages had been settled for decades. Nicolls then joined British troops on the Atlantic Coast. Left behind at Prospect Bluff were armed warriors and escaped slaves with the arsenal that Nicolls had previously deposited at the fortification that the Americans were now calling Negro Fort. To eliminate that sanctuary, General Jackson ordered General Edmund P. Gaines to destroy the fort, although the action would constitute an invasion of Spanish Florida. On July 27, 1816, Negro Fort was destroyed and its approximately 300 black and Indian defenders were killed or captured.

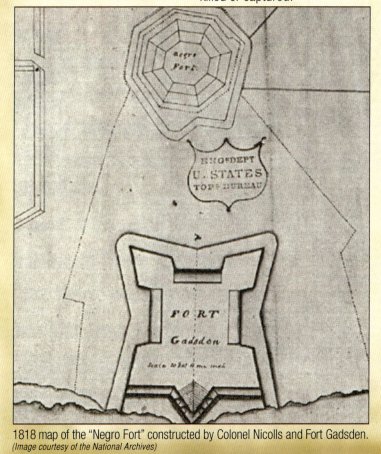

1818 map of the "Negro Fort" constructed by Colonel Nicolls and Fort Gadsden.
(Image courtesy of the National Archives)

North Central Region

Alachua County

Gainesville

🏛 P.K. Yonge Library of Florida History, University of Florida

Murphree Way
352.273.2755
uflib.ufl.edu/spec/pkyonge

Located in the 1925 Smathers Library building (formerly Library East), the P.K. Yonge Library in the Special and Area Studies Collections includes a vast array of books, maps, photographs, manuscripts, newspapers, and other materials documenting the state's history.

In the 1980s the P.K. Yonge Library began systematically microfilming Florida colonial records in the United States and Europe, including Britain, and assembled a comprehensive collection of documents pertaining to British history in the state. The Joseph Byrne Lockey Documents Collection includes transcripts and photocopies of numerous documents from the British Public Records Office relating to British East and West Florida, as well as British activities in the state during the Second Spanish Period. The Library's Florida Historical Map Collection contains over 280 maps dating to the British Period, including originals and reproductions of maps held by other institutions such as the British Public Records Office.

Micanopy

"William Bartram (1739 – 1823)" State Historical Marker

140 Block of Northeast Cholokka Boulevard

In 1962, a State Historical Marker was erected in present-day Micanopy regarding the travels of the naturalist William Bartram in this area. The text reads: "The great Quaker naturalist of Philadelphia made a long journey through the southeastern states in the 1770's collecting botanical specimens. In May, 1774, he visited the Seminole Chief, Cowkeeper, at

Map of the Southern British Colonies, 1776.
(Image courtesy of the State Archives of Florida)

North Central Region

the Indian village of Cuscowilla located near this spot. His book, "TRAVELS...", provided the earliest reliable account of North Florida landscape, flora, fauna and Indian life and his vivid images of local scenes inspired Coleridge, Wordsworth and Emerson."

DIXIE COUNTY

Horseshoe Beach

JACKSON WATER HOLE PARK
County Road 351

This small park, about 3 miles from Horseshoe Beach, was dedicated by the Dixie County Historical Society in 1997 to commemorate the invasion of Spanish Florida in 1818, during the First Seminole War, by an American force commanded by General Andrew Jackson. It is said to be the site of two wells dug by Jackson's troops. After seizing the fort at St. Marks, Jackson's force proceeded through this area to attack Indian villages near the Suwannee River. It was also in this area that Robert Armbrister, a British adventurer living among the Indians, was captured. Armbrister was taken to St. Marks and executed by the Americans, along with another British subject, Alexander Arbuthnot.

A State Historical Marker for "The Jackson Trail" is located in the park. The text reads: "On December 26, 1817, U.S. Secretary of War John C. Calhoun directed General Andrew Jackson to protect citizens trying to settle in Florida. Jackson arrived in Florida with the largest army ever to invade the state to date -- 2,000 Creek Warriors and 1,000 Georgia and Tennessee militiamen. After leaving Nashville, Tennessee, they traveled through Georgia and on to Florida, winding up in Suwannee-Old Town (now Dixie County). Jackson's goal was to remove the Indians, destroy their homes and confiscate their horses, cattle and food and slaves. In four days he had killed or driven off all Indians and escaped slaves. Near this spot, in April 1818, while on a "seek and find" mission, Jackson and his army captured Indian traders Robert Armbrister and Alexander Arbuthnot. They were British subjects who were supposed to be protected by a truce between England and the United States. Jackson had Arbuthnot hanged and Armbrister shot, which almost caused a war between the two countries. The Jackson Trail ran alongside Highway 19, branching south to the coast on the west side of what is now the Horseshoe Beach Road (Highway 351)." Although the marker indicates that Arbuthnot was also captured in this area, he was actually captured at St. Marks.

Old Town

"OLDTOWN" STATE HISTORICAL MARKER
US 19 and County Road 349

A second State Historical Marker in Dixie County also relates to the capture of British subject Robert Armbrister in this area by an American force during the First Seminole War. The text reads:

"Inhabited by the Upper Creeks, Oldtown, often called Suwanee Oldtown, was one of the largest Indian villages in northern Florida. In Andrew Jackson's punitive expedition into Florida in April, 1818, Oldtown was captured. Most of the renegade Indians escaped, but Jackson caught Robert Armbrister, a British subject, who was tried and executed for aiding the Creeks in border raids into Georgia. This produced tension between the United States and Great Britain."

LEON COUNTY

Tallahassee

 GOODWOOD MUSEUM AND GARDENS
1600 Miccosukee Road
850.877.4202
goodwoodmuseum.org

Goodwood was established in the 1830s by the Croom family of North Carolina who moved to the Territory of Florida to start several plantations in the region. By the mid-1840s, the large and ornate main house at Goodwood with its frescoed

The main house at Goodwood.
(Image courtesy of Goodwood Museum and Gardens)

North Central Region

ceilings had been completed, and it is today one of the finest surviving antebellum homes in North Florida. The crippling economic depression of the 1870s forced the owners of Goodwood to sell most of their land. In 1885, the Goodwood main house and remaining 160 acres were purchased by an Englishman, Dr. William L. Arrowsmith, who completed the transformation of the property from an agricultural enterprise to a country estate. Arrowsmith was a London civil engineer who, in 1841, was appointed Superintendent of Government Works in the British colony of Malta. In 1849, he was appointed Collector of Customs for Malta. He subsequently underwent medical training and is rumored to have been a personal doctor to Giuseppe Garibaldi, the military hero of Italian unification. In the 1860s, Arrowsmith moved to Philadelphia to practice medicine and teach at a medical college. After returning to England for several years, he moved back to the United States and purchased Goodwood. Arrowsmith died in 1886 but his English-born widow continued to live at Goodwood until she sold the property in 1911. After the death of the last owner in 1990, Goodwood was bequeathed to a foundation for use as a historic house museum and public park. Many of the paintings and furnishings still in the house were brought there from England by the Arrowsmiths.

Museum of Florida History
R.A. Gray Building
500 South Bronough Street
850.245.6400
museumoffloridahistory.com

The Museum of Florida History collects, preserves, exhibits, and interprets evidence of past and present cultures in Florida. As the state history museum, it focuses on artifacts unique to the role Florida has played in America's history. A permanent British Period exhibit includes topics relating to the 1781 Battle of Pensacola, the British-Indian trade network, and Andrew Turnbull's New Smyrna colony. Highlights include artifacts excavated from Fort George in Pensacola, British trade beads, and a circa 1760s British drop-front desk. In addition, significant British colonial artifacts in the Museum's collection include a rare finely-carved powder horn with scrimshaw-style images of St. Augustine buildings on one side and a meeting, probably the 1765 Treaty of Picolata conference, between the British and Native Americans on the other, and also an 18th century oil portrait of George Johnstone, the first British governor of West Florida (1763–1767).

State Library of Florida/ State Archives of Florida
R.A. Gray Building
500 South Bronough Street
850.245.6600
dlis.dos.state.fl.us/library

The Florida Collection in the State Library contains one of the most comprehensive holdings of Floridiana in the state. Books, manuscripts, maps, memorabilia, newspaper articles, and periodicals are among the 60,000 items in the collection housed in the Dorothy Dodd Room. The State Archives of Florida is the central repository for state government documents. In addition to official state records, it collects, preserves, and makes available for research private manuscripts, local government records, photographs, maps, and other Florida materials. Among the British related items in this collection are originals, photocopies, and microfilm of documents relating to British West Florida including the 1781 Battle of Pensacola, as well as original documents regarding the training of Royal Air Force pilots in Florida during World War II. The State Library's Florida Photographic Collection contains many images related to the British in Florida which are available online through their website, floridamemory.com.

WAKULLA COUNTY
St. Marks

Fort St. Marks, San Marcos de Apalache Historic State Park
148 Old Fort Road
850.925.6216
floridastateparks.org/sanmarcos

Beginning in 1679, the Spanish built two wooden forts at the

The trial of British subject Robert Armbrister at St. Marks, 1818.
(Image courtesy of the State Archives of Florida)

North Central Region

confluence of the St. Marks and Wakulla Rivers. In 1739, they began construction of the permanent stone fort of San Marcos de Apalache at the site. This stone fort was still under construction when the British acquired Florida in 1763. The half-completed fort, now called Fort St. Marks, was garrisoned by a British force of 56 men and armed with several cannons. However, a hurricane in October 1766 with a twelve foot storm surge caused considerable damage to the fort and resulted in a reduction of the garrison to 20 soldiers. In 1769, the British garrison was withdrawn and the fort was turned over to an Indian trading firm which maintained a store there.

During the Second Spanish Period, the fort was again occupied by Spanish troops but their control was threatened on several occasions. In 1800, the fort was captured by a force of mostly Creek and Seminole Indians led by the Maryland-born British colonial adventurer William Augustus Bowles, who had served in a British Loyalist regiment at Pensacola during the American Revolution. A Spanish military expedition from Pensacola recaptured the fort a month later. In 1818, during the First Seminole War, an American force commanded by General Andrew Jackson invaded Spanish Florida to punish the Indians there for border raids into the United States and for harboring escaped American slaves. Jackson's force seized the fort at St. Marks and captured Alexander Arbuthnot, a British merchant and Indian trader. The American troops then attacked Indian villages near the Suwannee River and, in the process, captured Robert Armbrister, a British adventurer living with the Seminoles. Armbrister was taken to St. Marks where both he and Arbuthnot were tried by an American military court on charges of inciting the Indians to hostilities against the United States. Both men were found guilty and executed by the Americans. Arbuthnot was hanged and Armbrister was shot by a firing squad. The execution of these two British subjects elicited outrage in Great Britain, but the British government decided against issuing a formal protest.

For the remainder of the Second Spanish Period and continuing after the American acquisition of Florida, American troops intermittently occupied the fort, which they called Fort St. Marks. During the Civil War, Confederate troops occupied the site and renamed it Fort Ward. The fort was abandoned following the war, and the property was acquired by the State of Florida in 1964 for use as a park facility. A visitor center and museum provides interpretation with exhibits and artifacts, and an interpretive trail runs through the site.

British St. Marks

Beginning in the late 1670s, the Spanish constructed a series of fortifications at the juncture of the St. Marks and the Wakulla rivers, south of Tallahassee near the Gulf of Mexico, first of wood and then of more durable stone. The British renamed Fort San Marcos de Apalache to Fort St. Marks when they took control of Florida in 1763.

James Pampellone, the commanding officer of the first British garrison, described the stone fort as having nine sides and nine angles, situated between two rivers, and surrounded by a ditch. Soldiers of the British 9th Regiment repaired the houses inside the fort and raised the walls three feet higher. George Swettenham, the fort's second commander, planted vegetables outside the fort's walls and encouraged soldiers to plant personal gardens to ensure a steady supply of provisions for the garrison.

The fort was damaged by a hurricane in October 1766 and quickly repaired by royal engineer James Moncrief. However, in 1769, General Thomas Gage, commander-in-chief of British forces in North America, responded to a directive from the War Department in London to cut military spending in the American colonies by ordering withdrawal of the garrisons at St. Marks and Picolata in East Florida and Natchez and Iberville in West Florida. Governor Grant warned of possible wars in the future and argued persuasively that the forts in East Florida should be maintained, not dismantled.

With Gage's approval, Grant issued a license to Charleston merchant John Gordon permitting him to establish an Indian trade store at St. Marks in return for maintaining the walls and buildings. A similar permit was arranged for Fort Picolata on the St. Johns River. By September 1769, Daniel McMurphy was at Fort St. Marks supplying the resident British traders who bargained with Native Americans for the deerskins and furs gathered on their annual hunts. Governor Grant was confident that the arrangement would promote commerce and Creek migration, and enhance relations with the Creek and Seminole villages already established near St. Marks. After Spain entered the War of American Independence and captured the Gulf coast towns and forts in West Florida, Fort St. Marks was abandoned by the British.

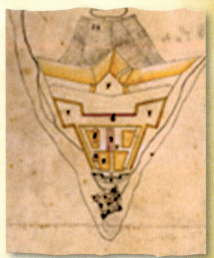

Map of Fort St. Marks, ca.1765.
(Image courtesy of the National Archives of the United Kingdom)

NORTHEAST REGION

CLAY COUNTY

Green Cove Springs

"Fort San Fransisco de Pupo" State Historical Marker
State Road 16 at Shands Bridge

The text of this marker reads: "Pupo is first mentioned in 1716 as the place where the trail from the Franciscan Indian Missions in Apalachee (present-day Tallahassee) to St. Augustine crossed the river. The Spanish government built the fort on the St. Johns River sometime before 1737. Pupo teamed with Fort Picolata on the Eastern Shore; these forts protected the river crossing and blocked ships from continuing upstream. In 1738 after an attack by the British-allied Yuchi Indians, the fort was enlarged to a 30-by-16 blockhouse, surrounded by a rampart of timber and earth. During General James Oglethorpe's 1739-40 advance on St. Augustine, Lt. George Dunbar unsuccessfully attacked Pupo on the night of December 28th. On January 7th and 8th, Oglethorpe himself took two days to capture the Spanish blockhouses. Oglethorpe reinforced the fort with a trench, which is still visible. Upon the British retreat from Florida, Fort San Fransisco de Pupo was destroyed. Though the fort was never rebuilt, the site remained a strategically important ferry crossing. In the 1820s, Florida's first federally built road, the Bellamy Road, used the river crossing on the route between St. Augustine and Pensacola."

South Carolina Governor James Moore Invades Spanish Florida in 1702 and 1704

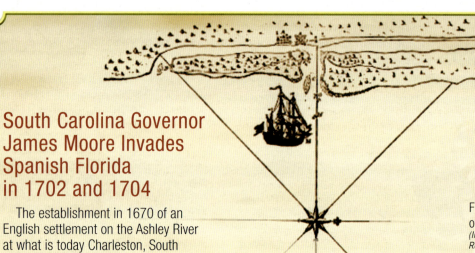

French map of Moore's attack on St. Augustine, 1702.
(Image courtesy of the University of North Carolina Research Laboratories of Archaeology)

The establishment in 1670 of an English settlement on the Ashley River at what is today Charleston, South Carolina, posed a grave danger to Spanish Florida. By 1690, the English colony had an expanding population, a prospering economy, and expansive trade networks with Native Americans. The Carolinians had also armed Native American allies and instigated raids on Guale, Timucua, and Apalachee villages and on Franciscan missions in Florida, posing a serious threat to the survival of Spanish Florida. That threat intensified when Spain and England were on opposite sides of the Queen Anne's War in 1701-1714 (known in Europe as the War of Spanish Succession).

In November 1702, Carolina governor James Moore raised an army of 1,200 men, primarily Creek warriors, and led an invasion of Spanish Florida. Moore and the main army traveled to St. Augustine aboard ships, while a detachment under Colonel Robert Daniel destroyed villages and missions on Amelia and Fort George Islands, crossed the St. Johns River to attack the mission village of Piritiriba on Pablo River, and marched south torching farms and ranches along the way.

Spanish governor José de Zúñiga y Cerda moved 1,700 soldiers and civilians inside Castillo de San Marcos, the stone fortress completed seven years before. When the fortress proved impregnable to English forces, Moore laid down a siege, expecting to starve the inhabitants into submission. The Spaniards rationed their corn and meat supplies and prayed for reinforcements.

A relief force from Havana arrived December 26th, trapping Moore's ships. In January 1703, Moore ordered his men to torch the houses, churches, and government buildings in the town, and march north to the St. Johns River to board ships and return to South Carolina. Fewer than two dozen buildings were left standing in St. Augustine.

One year later, now ex-governor Moore led an army of Carolina militia and Creek and Yamassee warriors on another invasion of Florida, focused on the area that is today Tallahassee. Spanish ranches and farms and Apalachee villages and provisions fields were destroyed; Mission San Luis was reduced to ashes. The invaders killed or enslaved several thousand Apalachee men, women and children. Raids by the Creek and Yamassee warriors continued for years, driving the few survivors into refugee villages outside the walls of St. Augustine. Spain's La Florida colony was reduced to a tiny enclave surrounding the protective walls of the Castillo de San Marcos.

Northeast Region

The "Dames Point Bridge," an Iconic British-era Place Name

For more than 230 years, a prominent location along the lower St. Johns River in Duval County has been called Dames Point by the residents of northeast Florida, although most people living there today cannot explain the origin of the place-name. When a bridge was completed in 1989 to connect Jacksonville's Arlington neighborhood and the location popularly known as Dames Point, it was officially named the Napoleon Bonaparte Broward Bridge, after a Duval County native who was the governor of Florida from 1905-1909. However, the official name never caught on with the public; it continues to be known as the Dames Point Bridge, after a British Loyalist refugee who resided in Florida for only four years.

The popular name for the bridge has its origins in the British colonial years in Florida, when John Cross was granted a 300-acre tract at a point of land jutting into the St. Johns River twelve miles from its merger with the Atlantic. The tract, known briefly as "Crosses Point," was purchased in 1780 by British Loyalist Charles Dames, a shipbuilder and ship captain engaged in the West Indies trade. Dames constructed dwellings for himself and nine slaves, a ship building facility, storehouses, and a large wharf to berth ships carrying timber and naval stores from Florida to the British Caribbean islands. After East Florida was ceded to Spain, Dames abandoned his property in 1784 and relocated to New Providence Island in the Bahamas.

Today, the northern footings for the Napoleon Bonaparte Broward Bridge are located on the point of land once owned by Charles Dames. But if locals are asked the name of the massive bridge looming nearby, the answer will likely be the "Dames Point Bridge."

Aerial photograph of "Dames Point Bridge" by Michael J. Canella.
(Image courtesy of Dr. Daniel Schafer, University of North Florida)

DUVAL COUNTY
Jacksonville

Delius House
Dolphin Drive
Jacksonville University
904.256.7000
ju.edu

The noted English composer Frederick Delius (1862-1934) was born in northern England to a prosperous mercantile family and, despite his musical inclinations, went to work in the family business. In 1884, he came to Florida to manage an orange plantation on the east bank of the St. Johns River at Solano Grove in St. Johns County. During his year and a half stay here, he increasingly concentrated his efforts on composing music, including taking lessons from a Jacksonville musician. He was also influenced by the singing, especially of spirituals, of the African American workers on his plantation.

In 1885, Delius moved to Virginia to pursue his now-wholly musical career. In 1886, he returned to Europe where he would live for the remainder of his life, mostly in France, and have a long and illustrious career as a musical composer. Among his musical compositions was the *Florida Suite*, an orchestral work inspired by his time at Solano Grove.

In 1961, the Delius home at Solano Grove was moved to the campus of Jacksonville University where it was restored for use as a Delius museum, and is open for tours by appointment. The Carl S. Swisher Library at Jacksonville University holds an archive of Delius' works, including some original scores. The University also held an annual Delius Festival for many years in honor of the composer although it has not been held for the last several years. In 1992, the Delius Association of Florida dedicated a monument at the site where the Delius home originally stood at Solano Grove. The monument consists of an irregular coquina block with a bronze bas-relief bust of Delius and a bronze plaque with information on Delius' time in Florida attached to it.

English composer Frederick Delius.
(Image courtesy of the State Archives of Florida)

Northeast Region

"Historic King's Road British East Florida" Historical Marker
Friendship Fountain, Museum Drive

The text of this marker reads: "The King's Road, built by the British prior to the American Revolution, began at the St. Mary's River, passed through Cowford (Jacksonville), crossed the St. John's River, it is believed, at present day Liberty Street, approximately one mile east of this marker, and continued south to New Smyrna. During the Revolution, American troops used this route to make attacks on British forces. The most notable of these engagements was at Alligator Creek Bridge, 30 June 1778. Following this battle the invasion of Florida by American troops ceased." This marker was erected in 1996 by the Florida State Society of the Daughters of the American Revolution.

King's Road Monument, Jacksonville.
(Image courtesy of Vale Fillmon, Florida State Historical Marker Program)

King's Road Monument
Northeast corner of Hemming Plaza

In 1928, the Jacksonville Chapter of the Daughters of the American Revolution (DAR) erected a small monument commemorating the King's Road in downtown Jacksonville. The monument consists of a coquina slab with an attached bronze plaque decorated with an outline map of Florida, two palm trees, and the DAR symbol. The plaque reads "At this spot the Kings Road met the Apalache Trail, so connecting the English colonies and the Spanish settlements of the West with St. Augustine and New Smyrna."

British Period exhibit at the Museum of Science and History, Jacksonville.
(Image courtesy of the Museum of Science and History)

Museum of Science and History
1025 Museum Circle
904.396.6674
themosh.org

The mission of the Museum of Science and History is to increase knowledge and understanding of the natural environment and history of Jacksonville and northeast Florida. A permanent exhibit, titled "Currents of Time," presents 12,000 years of regional history, including the British Period. It includes displays with dioramas and period artifacts relating to British East and West Florida, British plantations, and the American Revolution.

"Site of Cow Ford" State Historical Marker
Corner of East Bay Street and South Liberty Street

The text of this marker reads: "This narrow part of the St. Johns River, near a clear freshwater spring, was a crossing point for Indians and early travelers. The Indian name Wacca Pilatka, meaning "Cow's Crossing," was shortened by the English to Cow Ford, and Jacksonville was known by this name for many years. This crossing was used by the English when they made an old Timucuan Indian Trail into King's Road."

This location was used as a river crossing site by Native Americans and the Spanish prior to the British Period, and around 1740 the Spanish constructed a small fortification, Fort St. Nicholas, on the south side of the river to protect the crossing. During the British Period, this location was an important connecting point on the King's Road where flatboat ferries carried travelers across the St. Johns River. Too deep to ford by wading, cattle crossed the river by swimming or were transported by ferry at this point, leading to the designation of the area as Cowford (sometimes referred to as Cow Ford). Cowford was the site of a conference held in 1775 between the British and Florida Native Americans to solidify their alliance. During the American Revolution, the British erected a redoubt at Cowford which was garrisoned by a small detachment of British army regulars. In 1822, the area was renamed Jacksonville in honor of Andrew Jackson, the first American military governor of Florida.

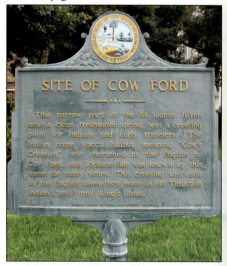

State Historical Marker for Cow Ford.
(Image courtesy of Vale Fillmon, Florida State Historical Marker Program)

Northeast Region

Mandarin

Mandarin Museum and Historical Society (Mandarin Store and Post Office)

11964 Mandarin Road
904.268.0784
mandarinmuseum.net

The Mandarin Museum & Historical Society preserves buildings, artifacts and documents related to the history of Mandarin and the lower St. Johns River basin area. During the British Period, Mandarin Point was the site of the 10,000 acre Julianton Plantation granted to Francis Levett, Sr., a wealthy merchant who had moved to East Florida from London. Here, Levett constructed an opulent home and formal gardens modeled after English country manors. The plantation's vast agricultural enterprise, operated by enslaved Africans, included extensive indigo, rice and vegetable fields, a peach orchard, orange groves, vineyards, and naval stores. Following the Spanish reacquisition of Florida in 1783, the Levett family abandoned the plantation and relocated to the Bahamas and eventually Georgia.

During the 1870s to 1890s, dozens of British families moved to the Mandarin area to participate in the citrus industry. Among these new settlers was Walter Jones, a native of Liverpool, England. In addition to his involvement in the citrus industry, Jones managed the town's general store which also served as the post office following his appointment as postmaster. In 1994, the City of Jacksonville acquired the property where Jones and his family had lived since the early 1900s and entered into an agreement with the Mandarin Museum & Historical Society to operate it as an historical park. The Walter Jones Historical Park contains a restored 1875 farmhouse, an 1876 barn, other historic structures which have been relocated to the park, and the Mandarin Museum building which opened in 2004. The nearby 1911 Mandarin Store and Post Office building, of which Jones was the proprietor and postmaster, is also operated as a museum by the Mandarin Museum & Historical Society.

Rice Cultivation at Governor James Grant's Mount Pleasant Plantation

Rice was cultivated at many British East Florida estates between 1763 and 1784. It never rivaled indigo as a commercial crop during the first decade of British rule in Florida, nor was it as profitable and extensive as naval stores production became after 1775. It is probable, however, that rice would have become an increasingly significant export crop if the British had retained control of East Florida at the conclusion of the American War of Independence. One such example of successful rice cultivation was at Governor James Grant's Mount Pleasant Plantation.

Between 1780 and 1782 slaves from Governor Grant's indigo plantation north of St. Augustine were moved 14 miles further north to create a new plantation at the headwaters of Guana River. Only a sand dune separated this site from the Atlantic Ocean, but it contained a mix of high and dry land and low marsh fed by fresh water. In seven months, 50 black men and women cleared the trees and brush from 120 acres of high ground, built log cabins, planted corn and indigo fields, and completed most of the ditching for a rice field. The workers next blocked the brackish water that pushed ahead of the ocean tides by compacting an earthen barrier at the south end of what would become the rice field. One mile to the north they compacted an upper dam which created a 1,000-acre fresh water holding pond to flood the rice field. The workers also dug ditches that alternately drained and fed fresh water to the rice plants.

On January 12, 1782, Dr. David Yeats, James Grant's agent in East Florida, pronounced the rice experiment a success. Rice plantations in Florida were expensive to initiate because of the labor intensity required, but once established they would continue to produce two cuttings of rice each year for as long as the dams and canals were kept intact and the fields maintained. In 1784, with the end of the British Period, the enslaved men and women who created Mount Pleasant disassembled their cabins for shipment to New Providence Island. Grant's slaves accompanied the cabins to the Bahamas, but were sent from there to South Carolina and sold to rice planters located at Santee River.

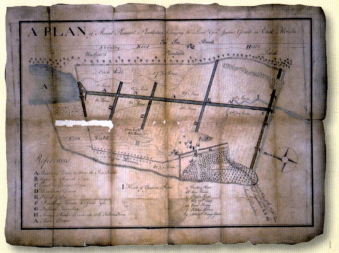

Map of Mount Pleasant Plantation, 1783.
(Image courtesy of the National Archives of the United Kingdom)

Northeast Region

"Incident at Thomas Creek" Battle of Thomas Creek, May 1777.
(Artist: Jackson Walker, Image courtesy of the Florida National Guard)

The War of American Independence and Loyal East Florida

East Florida's second governor, Patrick Tonyn, had been in the province for barely a year when the first shots of the American Revolution were fired in Massachusetts in 1775. Working in concert with John Stuart, superintendent of Indian affairs, Tonyn negotiated a treaty and alliance with the Seminole and the Creek, and ordered a census of trustworthy men fit to bear arms. By August 1776, he had formed the East Florida Rangers, a provincial militia of seven companies of white volunteers and four companies of enslaved black men serving under white officers. Command of the Rangers was assigned to Thomas Brown, a Loyalist refugee who had been tarred and feathered by rebels in Georgia before seeking refuge in East Florida.

The war in East Florida devolved into a series of violent plundering border raids that turned the area between the St. Marys and the St. Johns Rivers into a wasteland. Georgia militia crossed into Florida to destroy settlements and steal cattle and slaves, and the East Florida Rangers retaliated with raids into Georgia. Following Patriot raids in 1776, East Florida forces crossed into Georgia in February 1777, captured Fort McIntosh on the Satilla River and returned to St. Augustine with 2,000 head of cattle and 68 prisoners. A Georgia invasion force struck back in May but was stopped short of the St. Johns River at Thomas Creek.

In March 1778, the East Florida Rangers invaded Georgia to burn Fort Barrington on the Altamaha River. An American force of 2,000 retaliated in June, driving the Rangers south to the Alligator Creek Bridge on Nassau River, where the Americans were defeated by the Rangers and British regulars.

Reinforcements of British soldiers were rushed to St. Augustine in the summer of 1778. Under command of General Augustine Prevost, the army crossed the Florida/Georgia border and marched north to force the surrender of Savannah. Thus shielded on the north, the threat of invasion from Georgia was ended.

British General Augustine Prevost.
(Image courtesy of the State Archives of Florida)

FLAGLER COUNTY

Bunnell

"King's Road" State Historical Marker
Old King's Road near Princess Place Preserve Entrance

The text of this marker reads: "This road was built about 1766 when Colonel James Grant was governor of British East Florida. It extended from St. Augustine to Cowford (Jacksonville) and north to Colerain, Ga., across the St. Marys River. Later the road was extended south along the Matanzas River. Aided in part by donations from Grant's friends in South Carolina and Georgia, the road's chief financial backing came from local subscribers. It became a major artery of travel."

NASSAU COUNTY

Callahan

Battle of Thomas Creek State Historical Marker
US Highway 1 at Thomas Creek

Sometimes referred to as the southernmost land battle of the American Revolution, the 1777 Battle of Thomas Creek took place in northeast Florida near Thomas Creek, a tributary of the Nassau River. In response to a British raid from East Florida into Georgia in early 1777, the Americans organized an expedition to capture St. Augustine, the capital of East Florida. Under the overall command of Colonel Samuel Elbert, the invasion force consisted of some 400 Continental army troops sailing to Amelia Island by ship and about 150 Georgia militia cavalry traveling overland led by Colonel John Baker.

NORTHEAST REGION

Continental Army Colonel Samuel Elbert.
(Image courtesy of Hargrett Rare Book and Manuscript Library, University of Georgia)

Governor Patrick Tonyn and the Treaty Oak Congress of 1775

With a war of rebellion underway in the colonies north of East Florida, Governor Patrick Tonyn worried that his loyal province was ill-prepared to stop an invading army. Seeking allies, the governor invited Creek and Seminole headmen to a congress scheduled for December 4, 1775 at Fort Picolata. Tonyn waited anxiously at Picolata unaware that heavy rains had turned roads to mud and forced the Indians to take lengthy alternate routes that tired their horses. When the governor learned that a large number of headmen had gathered at the Cowford, the ferry landing at the south bank of the St. Johns River 40 miles north of St. Augustine, he and Indian Superintendent John Stuart hurried there to convene a historic congress.

Unlike previous congresses that focused on peace, justice, and land negotiations, the purpose of the 1775 meeting was to secure the allegiance of the Creek and

Native American leader Long Warrior, drawing by William Bartram.
(Image courtesy of the State Archives of Florida)

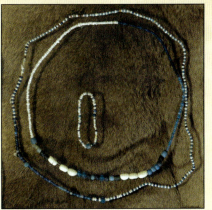

European glass beads made for trade to the Native Americans.
(Image courtesy of the Florida Division of Historical Resources)

the Seminole to His Majesty's side during the American Revolution. Indian leaders Pumpkin King and the Long Warrior were treated to a cruise on the British ship *St. Lawrence*, and were given commissions as "Captains of their Towns."

The congress closed with distribution of weapons and gun powder. Although it was contrary to his official instructions, Tonyn loaned supplies of gun powder from Fort St. Mark in St. Augustine to the Indian trader William Panton, who in turn passed them on to the Creek and Seminole leaders. Well-armed Indian allies would soon be needed to repel invaders from Georgia and to conduct border warfare. Tonyn's achievement was the forging of alliances that endured throughout the War of American Independence.

According to local legend, the congress was held near the ferry landing under the boughs of a live oak tree that subsequently became known as the Treaty Oak. While the legend cannot be definitively proven, a giant live oak stands today in the Jesse Ball duPont Park on Prudential Drive in South Jacksonville, close by the site of the 1775 ferry landing. The tree is over 70 feet tall, with a circumference exceeding 25 feet and a crown span of 145 feet. Foresters in several states have determined that Southern live oaks can live well beyond 500 years.

However, Elbert's main force was delayed in reaching the rendezvous point with Baker. Before Elbert could arrive, Baker's militia was attacked on May 17, 1777 by a British force of some 200 men including army regulars commanded by Major James Mark Prevost, Loyalist militia known as the East Florida Rangers led by Lieutenant Colonel Thomas Brown, and their Indian allies who were primarily Creeks. The American force was completely routed. Casualty reports vary with between 3 and 9 Americans reported killed, 9 wounded, and between 30 and 40 captured. Of the American prisoners, approximately half were later killed by the Indians in retaliation for the killing and mutilation of one of their members in an earlier skirmish. The British did not report any casualties. Upon learning of the defeat and low on provisions, Elbert abandoned the invasion and returned to Georgia. In 1975, a State Historical Marker for the "Battle of Thomas Creek" was erected on US Highway 1 south of Callahan in Nassau County. Although the exact location of the battlefield is unknown, it is believed to be south of Thomas Creek in Duval County in the Thomas Creek Preserve section of the Timucuan Ecological and Historic Preserve.

NORTHEAST REGION

BATTLE OF ALLIGATOR CREEK BRIDGE HISTORICAL MARKER
US Highway 1 between C.R.115 and C.R. 106

Following the American defeat at the Battle of Thomas Creek in 1777, the British in East Florida resumed raids into Georgia from their base at Fort Tonyn on the St. Marys River near Mills Ferry. In 1778, the Americans planned a second and larger invasion of East Florida with a combined force of Continental Army troops commanded by Major General Robert Howe, Georgia militia commanded by Governor John Houstoun, and South Carolina militia commanded by Colonel Andrew Williamson which totaled some 2,000 men. An important goal of the campaign was the capture of Fort Tonyn which was defended by the Loyalist East Florida Rangers militia and their Indian allies commanded by Lieutenant Colonel Thomas Brown. As the American troops entered East Florida, the British defenders evacuated Fort Tonyn and the Americans occupied the abandoned fort on June 29, 1778. Brown withdrew towards a defensive position prepared by British army regulars under the command of Major James Mark Prevost at Alligator Creek Bridge, about 17 miles south of Fort Tonyn. Brown was pursued by a detachment of about 100 Georgia militia cavalry commanded by General James Screven which attacked the British position manned by several hundred troops at Alligator Creek Bridge on June 30, 1778. In the ensuing battle, the Americans were repulsed with more than 13 killed and several wounded. The British suffered one killed and several wounded, some of whom later died from their wounds. Following the defeat at Alligator Creek Bridge, the American force, wracked by dissension among its commanders and disease among its soldiers, called off its invasion attempt. In mid-July 1778, Fort Tonyn was destroyed and the Americans withdrew back to Georgia. There would be no further American attempts to capture East Florida during the American Revolution. In 1936, a historical marker commemorating the battle, entitled "Skirmish of American Revolution," was erected on US Highway 1 in Callahan at Alligator Creek by the Jacksonville Chapter of the Florida Society of the Sons of the American Revolution.

The King's Botanist: John Bartram and the St. Johns River in 1765-1766

In April 1765, King George III granted a stipend and the title of royal botanist to John Bartram, a 66-year-old Quaker from Pennsylvania, with the expectation that Bartram would explore Britain's new Florida provinces. Little was known about East and West Florida at the time, but already potential investors were clamoring for maps and information concerning the new colonies.

By October 11, Bartram and his son William Bartram were in St. Augustine, and on December 21, they launched a dugout canoe on an eight-week exploration of the St. Johns River, East Florida's most important waterway. They investigated both shores from the merger of the river with the Atlantic Ocean to Lakes Ruth and Loughman on the south, which they mistakenly assumed to be the river's headwaters. In all, the Bartrams traveled more than 500 miles.

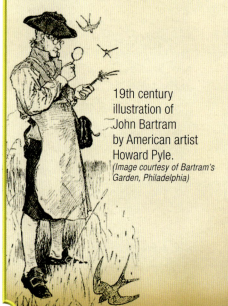
19th century illustration of John Bartram by American artist Howard Pyle.
(Image courtesy of Bartram's Garden, Philadelphia)

John Bartram.
(Image courtesy of the State Archives of Florida)

John recorded in his journal observations of East Florida's rivers and creeks, wetlands and savannahs, and oak and pine forests. He carefully documented shell bluffs and ridges, springs and natural flowing wells, "old fields" once planted in corn by Native Americans, ancient campsites strewn with broken Indian pots and other artifacts, live oak, magnolia, cypress and pine forests, and the numerous locations where fertile soil would support agriculture or grazing. The journal later served as a practical guide for future development; it is also an invaluable historical document that describes the St. Johns River valley before developers other than Native Americans altered its appearance.

John Bartram's journal was sent to London and was included in the second edition of Dr. William Stork's *A Description of East-Florida*, published in London in 1766. It was widely read in Britain and helped fan the flames of a "Florida Fever" that encouraged future British settlements in East Florida.

NORTHEAST REGION

Fernandina Beach

"Revolutionary War Invasion of British East Florida" Historical Marker
100 Block of Centre Street

The text of this marker reads: "In May 1777, Colonel Samuel Elbert's Continentals landed on the North End of Amelia Island at Oldtown Bluff, approximately one mile north of this marker, for a planned invasion of Florida. A patrol engaged in a skirmish with British troops on the south end of the island. An officer, Lt. Robert Ward, was killed and two of his soldiers were wounded. In retaliation, Col. Elbert ordered houses burned and the destruction of all cattle." This marker was erected in 1996 by the Florida State Society of the Daughters of the American Revolution.

PUTNAM COUNTY

Countywide

Putnam County Bartram Trail
bartram.putnam-fl.com

During his exploratory trips to British East Florida in the 1760s with his father and by himself in the 1770s, the noted naturalist William Bartram stopped at many locations in present-day Putnam County to explore or camp. The Putnam County Bartram Trail consists of biking, hiking, driving, and canoeing trails linking locations where Bartram visited. Thirty-one locations identified as Bartram's stopping places and campsites in the county are marked with signage. Informational kiosks relating to Bartram's travels are located at Palatka, Welaka, and Stokes Landing which was the site of Spalding's Lower Store during the British Period (see page 7). Based at St. Simon's Island in Georgia, James Spalding and his business associate Roger Kelsall operated several Indian trading stores in British East Florida. At Spalding's Lower Store, the firm constructed dwellings for their traders and storehouses for distributing trade goods to their other stores. For several months in 1774, Bartram used the Lower Store as his base while exploring this area and the traders there supplied him with lodging and logistical support. The Putnam County Bartram Trail website provides detailed descriptions of the 31 locations visited by Bartram, including historical summaries, journal and book entries by the Bartrams, maps, and links to additional resources.

The Travels of William Bartram

The noted American-born naturalist William Bartram first traveled to East Florida in 1764-1765 with his father, the royal botanist John Bartram. The trail they followed was not a land route; rather it was the St. Johns River from its merger with the Atlantic Ocean to Baxter Mound, 250 miles upriver (to the south). They traveled an undeveloped countryside with only five European settlements and three Indian trading stores.

William Bartram returned to East Florida in March 1774 as part of a 2,400 mile historic journey through the current states of North and South Carolina, Georgia, Florida, Alabama, Mississippi, Louisiana, and Tennessee. In Florida, Bartram traveled for eight months in a small sailboat, with additional horseback journeys to Seminole villages located inland from the St. Johns, recording his observations in a journal. After reuniting with his parents in 1777, William lived the rest of his life at his father's farm outside Philadelphia. He transformed his travel journals and memories into *Travels Through North and South Carolina, Georgia, East and West Florida,* published in 1791 and still in print in several editions and languages. The poetic beauty of Bartram's passages are the product of a natural philosopher contemplating God, man, and beauty in the exotic state of nature that Florida represented in his romantic imagination. For many generations *Travels* has been considered a literary and artistic masterpiece by readers throughout the world.

William Bartram portrait by Charles Willson Peale, 1808.
(Image courtesy of Independence National Historical Park)

William Bartram drawings of a green heron and a sandhill crane.
(Images courtesy of the Natural History Museum, London)

NORTHEAST REGION

East Palatka

"ROLLESTOWN" STATE HISTORICAL MARKER
US Highway 17 south of Caca Road

Denys Rolle, a wealthy British landowner and Member of Parliament, arrived in East Florida in 1764 to locate the site for an agricultural enterprise on a 20,000 acre land grant from the British government. He established a plantation at modern-day East Palatka which eventually grew to 78,000 acres from additional land grants and purchases. Rolle's vast estate of Rollestown, also known as Charlottia, stretched for 23 miles along the eastern side of the St. Johns River. He first tried using some 200 indentured workers recruited from English slums and jails to work his plantation in the belief that this opportunity for a new life would transform them into productive members of society. The experiment was a failure. Many of the workers vanished as soon as the ships arrived in Charleston, Savannah, or St. Augustine. The others quickly fled the plantation due to the harsh conditions of frontier life and bad management. Rolle subsequently purchased more than 200 enslaved Africans to take their place and produced turpentine, orange juice, cattle, rice, and indigo. Although Rolle periodically returned to England for prolonged periods, he continued to buy more property in East Florida, including a house and lot in St. Augustine. In 1780, Rolle purchased the 3,000-acre Jericho Plantation in today's South Jacksonville from James Penman and renamed it Chichester. After the transfer of Florida back to Spain in 1783, Rolle joined the British exodus and moved his enslaved workers to a 2,000-acre plantation in the Bahamas. A State Historical Marker for "Rollestown" was erected in 1961 in the area of his plantation at East Palatka.

Loyalist Refugees and St. Johns Town

The surrender of Lord Charles Cornwallis's army in Virginia in 1781 persuaded Britain to conduct peace negotiations to end the American Revolution. The rebellious American colonies were granted independence, and in June of 1782, East Florida was designated a haven for British Loyalists. Within six months, more than 6,000 refugees were transported to St. Augustine.

The refugees were provided emergency rations, tools, and seeds to plant at unoccupied rural tracts. The new settlers created hundreds of farms that produced food supplies, naval stores and lumber for export to Britain's Caribbean colonies. Seemingly overnight, a new town of between two and three hundred houses sprang up at St. Johns Bluff, a 300-acre tract located on the south bank of the St. Johns River, six miles from the Atlantic Ocean.

The bluff property was surveyed and 230 building lots were sold to refugees. Live oak trees were cut in the adjoining forests to supply a shipyard established by the tract's new owner, Thomas Williamson. Merchants opened stores at the waterfront and ship captains traveling downriver with cargoes of lumber and turpentine patronized the town's taverns and inns. Bakers, blacksmiths, and ship chandlers relocated to the new town to take advantage of the increased ship traffic. Many prominent Loyalists settled in the town. Governor Tonyn estimated that in just a few weeks more than 200 houses were built.

The hopes for future prosperity at St. Johns Town were dashed in January 1783 when British delegates in Paris agreed to preliminary terms of peace that ceded East and West Florida to Spain. Unwilling to live under Spanish governance, residents disassembled their buildings, hoping to use the boards again at new locations in the British West Indies.

Today, no above-ground traces of St. Johns Town can be found; the Loyalist settlement vanished as rapidly as it was constructed. Trees now grow on the hillside where streets were carved and houses once stood. Fort Caroline National Memorial, part of the National Park Service's Timucuan Ecological and Historic Preserve, occupies a large portion of the property.

Uniform buttons from a Loyalist regiment (left) and the 71st Regiment of Foot (right), recovered from a 1782 British shipwreck at St. Augustine.
(Image courtesy of the St. Augustine Lighthouse and Museum)

ST. JOHNS COUNTY

Palm Valley

"FORT SAN DIEGO (DIEGO PLAINS)" STATE HISTORICAL MARKER
200 Block of Landrum Lane

The text of this marker reads: "In 1736 Diego de Espinosa owned a cattle ranch on Diego Plains, a flat, open area east of here. For protection against Indians, his house was surrounded by a 15-foot high palisade with two bastions at opposite corners. Manned later by Spanish soldiers, this post was known at Fort San Diego. On May 23,

British gun flints from San Marcos de Apalache Historic State Park.
(Image courtesy of the Florida Division of Historical Resources)

NORTHEAST REGION

1740, during the British expedition against St. Augustine, General James Oglethorpe's 400 man army captured the fort and its 50 defenders. The British added a ditch and breastwork, and used the fort to protect the St. Johns River-St. Augustine supply line. They evacuated the fort on July 25. By 1743 it lay in ruins."

Picolata

"Picolata 'Pass of the Salamatoto River'" State Historical Marker
Intersection of State Road 13 and County Road

Located about 18 miles west of St. Augustine on the east bank of the St. Johns River (known as the Salamatoto River during much of the First Spanish Period), Picolata was a site of strategic importance throughout Florida's colonial history. The Spanish road from St. Augustine to the western provinces crossed the river via ferry at this point and Spanish troops were stationed here at least as early as 1680. In 1734, the Spanish constructed a wooden fort at this site and another, Fort San Fransisco de Pupo, across the river. Both forts were captured and destroyed by British forces during Georgia Governor James Oglethorpe's invasion of Spanish Florida in 1740. In the early 1750s the Spanish rebuilt Fort Picolata with a stone tower and wooden palisades.

During the British Period, the fort was initially maintained as a westerly outpost tied to St. Augustine by road and garrisoned by British troops. In 1765, East Florida Governor James Grant, Indian Superintendent John Stuart, and other British colonial officials convened a conference with the leading chiefs of the Florida Creeks at the fort. The resultant Treaty of Picolata defined the areas open in Florida for British settlement and those which were reserved for the Indians. A second British-Indian conference was held at the fort in 1767 to conduct negotiations for settling other issues. A number of farms and plantations were created by the British in the vicinity of Fort Picolata following the Indian conferences. The British army maintained an eight-man garrison at the fort until 1769 when they were withdrawn to St. Augustine. The fort was turned over to an Indian trading firm which maintained a store there. During the American Revolution, the fort was re-occupied by a British military detachment in the mid-1770s. After the British Period, the fort fell into disrepair although Picolata was the scene of military activities during the Patriot War of 1812, the Second Seminole War, and the Civil

The 1765 Treaty of Picolata

Establishing and maintaining peaceful relationships with the Native Americans in their respective provinces was a major challenge confronting governors George Johnstone and James Grant when they arrived in Florida late in 1764. The military commanders who had ruled the provinces until the governors arrived met with and distributed presents to the Indians of the region, and the governors hurried to do the same. In 1765, West Florida Governor Johnstone held congresses with leaders of the Chickasaw, Choctaw, Creek, Alabama and smaller tribes at Mobile and Pensacola that led to land concessions and peaceful relations, essential for a colony peopled by approximately 28,000 Indians and fewer than 3,000 British. Johnstone's abrupt change of attitude in 1766, when he repeatedly advocated a British war against the Creek, led to his dismissal as governor in February 1767.

In 1765, East Florida Governor James Grant sent representatives to the Creek towns throughout the southeast inviting the leaders to attend a congress at Fort Picolata, 20 miles west of St. Augustine on the St. Johns River. When the congress convened in November 1765, 50 Lower Creek and Seminole headmen met with Grant and John Stuart, Superintendent of Indian Affairs for the nations south of the Ohio River.

For Governor Grant, two major benefits resulted from the conference: confidence that peaceful relations between the British and the Native Americans would continue, and a land concession by the Creek chiefs that permitted English settlements to be formed south of the St. Marys River and its headwaters, and east of the St. Johns River. West of the St. Johns, settlements could be initiated as far inland as the tidal waters flowed. English settlers were assured that they could move to rural tracts without fear of attack by hostile Indian warriors.

Although tenacious concerning giving up their land to the British, the Creek and Seminole were assured by Governor Grant that his government would treat them fairly and exercise justice, and that Indian hunters could pass through English plantations when pursuing deer and other animals. The valuable hunting grounds remained open to the Creek and Seminole, and the governor pledged to regulate the British fur traders and to enhance opportunities for profitable exchanges.

Grant convened other meetings with Creek leaders in subsequent years, as did interim-Governor John Moultrie and the second British governor of East Florida, Patrick Tonyn. These meetings resulted in generally peaceful relations between the English and the Creek and Seminole throughout the British years in East Florida.

Map of Fort Picolata, 1765.
(Image courtesy of the State Archives of Florida)

NORTHEAST REGION

Indigo Cultivation at Governor James Grant's Villa Plantation

The main export crop in British East Florida during the 1760s and 1770s was indigo, a natural blue dye extracted from plants. The most profitable indigo plantation in the province was located at Governor James Grant's Villa Plantation, a 1,450-acre tract located approximately six miles northwest of St. Augustine. Grant, a native of Scotland, was appointed East Florida's first governor in 1763 and arrived at St. Augustine in August 1764.

Considering the entire province "as a great plantation put under my care," Governor Grant experimented with seeds and plants suitable for Florida's soil and climate at a 300-acre farm north of the city gate. He then established his highly successful Villa indigo plantation at the juncture of the Guana and North Rivers, for which he purchased 78 enslaved Africans to do the work. Beginning in 1768, Grant's enslaved Africans cleared 600 acres for indigo cultivation. Indigo weed was processed into dye in six sets of vats spread out among the fields. Structures at the plantation included two dwellings and a kitchen for the overseer and his assistants, stables for horses and other plantation work animals, blacksmith shop, large barn and indigo house, fowl and pigeon coops and houses for the enslaved black men and women.

After only four years, the profits from exports of indigo dye repaid all of his startup expenses, including the cost of the slaves. Grant's Villa was called an "agricultural college" by one observer, for the overseers who came there to observe cultivation and processing techniques and later applied them to their own estates. Indigo became East Florida's most profitable export crop.

East Florida Governor James Grant.
(Image courtesy of the State Archives of Florida)

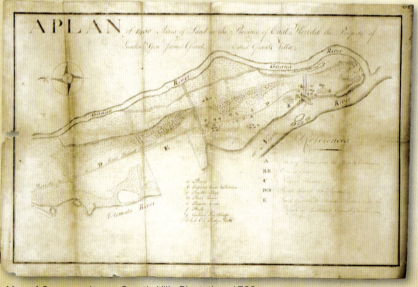

Map of Governor James Grant's Villa Plantation, 1783.
(Image courtesy of the National Archives of the United Kingdom)

War. The road from Picolata remained a major land route to St. Augustine until the railroad arrived in the late 19th century. In 1962, a State Historical Marker was placed at Picolata.

Ponte Vedra Beach

"Governor Grant's Plantations" State Historical Marker

Guana Tolomato Matanzas National Estuarine Research Reserve
505 Guana River Road

The text of this marker reads:
"In 1768, James Grant (1720-1806), Governor of British East Florida from 1763 to 1773, established Grant's Villa Plantation at the juncture of the Guana and North Rivers. Enslaved Africans cleared the 1,450-acre tract of land, planted indigo seeds, and processed the plants into blue indigo dye. Indigo dye became East Florida's main export, and Grant's Villa was its most profitable plantation. By 1780, due to declining soil fertility and the disruption of transportation routes during the American Revolution, indigo cultivation was no longer profitable. Ordered to develop a new estate 12 miles north at the headwaters of Guana River, overseer William Brockie and the slaves completed Mount Pleasant Plantation in 1781. Just south of today's Mickler Road, between SR A1A and Neck Road, the slaves built two earthen dams which enclosed a 220-acre rice field. The dam on the south blocked the flow of salty tidal water. The barricade to the north created a fresh water reservoir. In 1784, following the return of East Florida to Spain, both plantations were abandoned and the enslaved Africans were transported to The Bahamas, from where they were sold to rice planters in South Carolina."

NORTHEAST REGION

St. Augustine

AVERO HOUSE (ST. PHOTIOS GREEK ORTHODOX NATIONAL SHRINE)
41 St. George Street
904.829.8205
stphotios.com

This colonial structure, constructed in the 1740s during the First Spanish Period, is known not only for its long association with the Avero family, a prominent Spanish colonial family, but also for its use during the British Period as a Catholic church for Smyrnea Settlement refugees. After the collapse of Andrew Turnbull's settlement in nearby New Smyrna in 1777, many of the colony's indentured servants and laborers who had come from the Mediterranean area in 1768, mostly Minorcans but also Greeks and Italians, fled to St. Augustine. British East Florida Governor Patrick Tonyn appropriated the then-vacant house from real estate agent and speculator Jesse Fish and offered it to the Turnbull Colony's Catholic pastor, Father Pedro Camps, who established the Church of San Pedro in the building. Following the British Period, the building passed through a succession of owners until 1966 when it was purchased by the Greek Orthodox Diocese for use as a shrine and museum dedicated to this first Greek colony in America. Exhibits depict the life of the early Greeks in British Florida and elsewhere, as well as the history of the Greek Orthodox Church in America.

Governor James Oglethorpe of Georgia and the 1740 English Invasion of Spanish Florida

The establishment of the colony of Georgia in 1732 initiated a renewal of hostilities between Spanish Florida and the English settlements to the north. Claiming Mosquito Inlet (70 miles south of St. Augustine) as the southern boundary of Georgia, Governor James Edward Oglethorpe built a series of fortifications on the coastal islands that included Fort George Island, north of the inlet to the St. Johns River. In 1739, England declared war on Spain in what became the War of Jenkins' Ear and later was expanded as the War of Austrian Succession. Oglethorpe seized the opportunity to invade Spanish Florida in 1740. His troops captured Fort Picolata and Fort Pupo on the St. Johns River in January. Then, in May, Oglethorpe's force began marching southward from the south bank at the entrance to the river (today's Mayport), arriving at the outer walls of St. Augustine in early June. The British forces then surrounded St. Augustine, set up artillery placements and established siege lines.

Thirty-eight years after James Moore's army from Carolina had

"The Guns of Anastasia" British siege of St. Augustine, 1740.
(Artist: Jackson Walker, Image courtesy of the Legendary Florida Collection)

attempted to starve the Spaniards into submission, another British force attempted to do the same. Spanish Governor Manuel de Montiano crowded over 2,500 people inside the Castillo de San Marcos and prayed for relief ships from Havana. Oglethorpe set up an artillery camp north of St. Augustine Inlet and another on Anastasia Island, but the cannon balls that struck the walls of the fort bounced off or were absorbed by the soft coquina blocks.

In late June, with provisions running low, Governor Montiano ordered Spanish troops, including free black militia, to attack British troops encamped at Fort Mose north of town. Most of the British soldiers were killed or captured in a demoralizing event for Governor Oglethorpe. In early July, Montiano's prayers were answered. A relief force of seven Spanish ships arrived with provisions and troop reinforcements. Oglethorpe was forced to withdraw and return with his army to Georgia. Once again, the sturdy walls of the Castillo had proved to be impregnable.

NORTHEAST REGION

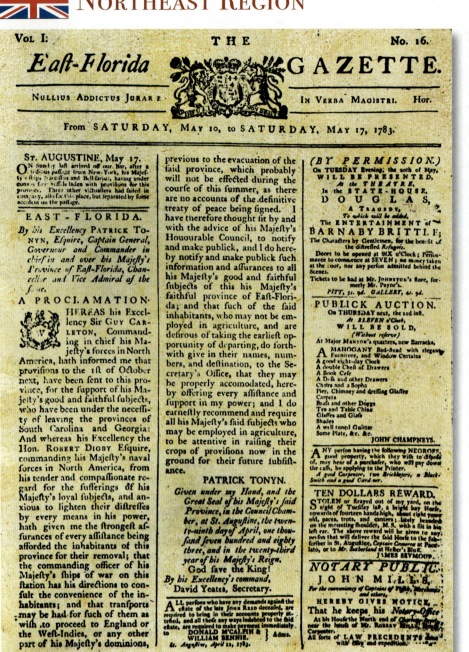

East Florida Gazette, Florida's first newspaper.
(Image courtesy of the State Archives of Florida)

De Mesa–Sanchez House
43 St. George Street
904.342.2857
colonialquarter.com/explore/british-18th-century

Constructed in the 1740s during the First Spanish Period, the house became the property of William Walton, a wealthy New York merchant, at the beginning of the British Period. Walton's export company had been contracted to supply the Spanish garrison at St. Augustine during much of the 1700s prior to the British acquisition of Florida. In the course of settling debts owed him by the departing Spanish, Walton accumulated considerable landholdings in St. Augustine. After Walton's death in 1768, this house reverted to the British Crown and, in 1771, East Florida Governor James Grant granted it to Joseph Stout. Stout had moved to East Florida from Philadelphia in 1767 to manage plantations owned by John Tucker in the area of present-day Welaka. In 1779, Stout purchased a tract on the Matanzas River south of St. Augustine where he established an indigo plantation. Although he spent most of his time on the plantations, Stout used this house in St. Augustine as his town home and offices. During the British Period, the De Mesa-Sanchez House was enlarged and improved. After the reacquisition of Florida by Spain, Stout left St. Augustine for the Bahamas where he established a cotton plantation.

The De Mesa-Sanchez House was subsequently owned by a series of private owners until 1976 when it was purchased by the Historic St. Augustine Preservation Board. The house is open to the public as part of the "18th Century British 14th Colony" section of the St. Augustine "Colonial Quarter" living history attraction. The British section of the Quarter also includes a small reconstructed wooden building containing a full sized reproduction of an 18th century printing press commemorating the *East Florida Gazette*, Florida's first newspaper, published in St. Augustine in 1783-1784. The "Bull and Crown Publick House," an interpretation of a British pub of the period, is located in another reconstructed building within the Quarter's British section.

Evergreen Cemetery
505 North Rodriguez Street
904.829.8771

Established in 1886 west of St. Augustine outside the city limits, Evergreen Cemetery was the largest Protestant cemetery in the region during the late 1800s and early 1900s. Among those buried here is Randolph Caldecott, the noted British illustrator of children's books for whom the prestigious Caldecott Medal is named. Born in 1846 in Chester,

Northeast Region

England, Caldecott was trained at the Manchester School of Art and became internationally famous for his illustrations in children's books which greatly influenced that genre of literature. In 1886, during a trip to the United States, Caldecott became ill and died at St. Augustine. His gravesite in the Evergreen Cemetery is maintained by the Randolph Caldecott Society of America. In 1937, the American Library Association created the Caldecott Medal to be awarded annually, beginning in 1938, to the artist of the most distinguished children's picture book published in the United States during the preceding year. A State Historical Marker at Evergreen Cemetery provides information on its history and funerary art.

Father Miguel O'Reilly House Museum
32 Aviles Street
904.826.0750
oreillyhouse.org

Originally constructed during the First Spanish Period, this house was acquired in 1772 during the British Period by James Penman, a wealthy merchant and planter. Penman arrived in East Florida in 1766 as the agent for a wealthy Englishman named Peter Taylor. The two men were partners in a venture to establish two plantations on the Mosquito River, 70 miles south of St. Augustine. The partnership dissolved in 1772 with Penman retaining an estate of 3,000 acres. Penman was also the owner of the 3,000-acre Jericho Plantation located on the east side of the St. Johns River in present-day South Jacksonville. Jericho Plantation was operated by 120 enslaved Africans and produced indigo, lumber, naval stores, rice, corn, and beans. Cattle, horses, pigs, and poultry were also raised there. Penman subsequently sold his house on Aviles Street to Jonathan Mowbray, a sea captain. During the American Revolution, Mowbray was put in command of the provincial marine service created by East Florida Governor Patrick Tonyn. His vessel, the armed sloop *Rebecca*, was engaged in several actions against the Americans. During an engagement at St. Simon's Island, Georgia in April 1778, the *Rebecca* ran aground and had to be abandoned. Although the *Rebecca* was captured by the Americans, Mowbray and his men escaped to another British ship. Mowbray was then given command of another vessel in the provincial service, the *Germain*. In 1785, after the return of Florida to Spain, Mowbray sold the house to Father Miguel O'Reilly, an Irish-born Catholic priest who served as a chaplain to the Spanish troops stationed in St. Augustine. The building has remained in religious use since that time. Since 1866, it has been occupied by the Sisters of St. Joseph who currently administer it as a house museum and archival repository.

Captain Robert Searles and the 1668 Buccaneer Raid on St. Augustine

A century after Sir Francis Drake sacked St. Augustine, another British attack caused similar destruction and death and prompted major changes. In 1668, a Jamaican-based buccaneer named Captain Robert Searles led a raid through the streets of St. Augustine. Searles and his men had distinguished themselves as privateers in previous raids, (privateers, similar to pirates, were licensed by governments to attack enemies during wars). They had ruthlessly attacked and plundered Spanish cities in the Americas when Spain and England were at war. During Anglo/Dutch wars in 1665 and 1666, Searles led raids at the Caribbean islands of St. Eustatius, Trinidad, and Tobago.

In 1668, it was St. Augustine that suffered at the hands of Searles and his band of 100 brigands. During a surprise midnight raid the British buccaneers plundered dwellings and the Spanish counting house. Some soldiers and civilians found safety in the city's wooden fort while others escaped to the woods, but at least 60 Spaniards were killed and others captured and held for ransom. Because of the Searles raid, and the threatening establishment of an English colony at Ashley River in South Carolina two years later, the Council of the Indies authorized funds for construction of a stone fort at St. Augustine. Construction began in 1672. The Castillo de San Marcos, built of coquina stone quarried at Anastasia Island was finally completed in 1695.

Illustration from the 1st edition of *Buccaneers of America*, 1678 by Alexandre Exquemelin.
(Image courtesy of the Library of Congress)

Northeast Region

Map of Oglethorpe's siege of St. Augustine, 1740.
(Image courtesy of the State Archives of Florida)

Fort St. Mark, Castillo de San Marcos National Monument

1 South Castillo Avenue
904.829.6506
nps.gov/casa

Following the sacking of St. Augustine by the English privateer Robert Searle in 1668 and the founding of Charles Towne (present-day Charleston) only two days sail away by the English in 1670, the Spanish began construction in 1672 of a massive stone fortification, the Castillo de San Marcos, for the protection of the city. Constructed of coquina quarried on nearby Anastasia Island, the fort was completed in 1695. Today, it is the only surviving 17th century military structure in the United States. Twice during the First Spanish Period, the fort was placed under siege by the British. In 1702, during Queen Anne's War, South Carolina Governor James Moore invaded Florida with a force of some 600 colonial militia and some 600 Indian allies. The Spanish garrison of some 200 men and about 1,500 civilians barricaded themselves in the Castillo and successfully withstood a British siege for almost two months, as British cannon had little effect on the coquina walls which absorbed the impact of the shells. With the arrival of Spanish reinforcements from Cuba, Moore abandoned the invasion, burned the city, and returned to South Carolina. In 1740, during the War of Jenkins' Ear, a force of some 1,500 British regulars, colonial militia and their Indian allies under the command of Georgia Governor James Oglethorpe supported by the British navy laid siege to St. Augustine. As in 1702, the Spanish force of some 750 men and about 2,000 civilians retreated to the Castillo, and the British siege guns located on Anastasia Island and present-day Vilano Beach had little effect on the fort's coquina

NORTHEAST REGION

walls. After a month of unsuccessful bombardment and with the approach of hurricane season, Oglethorpe raised the siege and withdrew to Georgia.

After the British acquisition of Florida in 1763, the Castillo was renamed Fort St. Mark. British troops made a series of improvements to the fort, including the construction of wooden second floors in its vaulted casements to provide more space for housing and supplies. During the American Revolution, the fort housed as many as 500 British soldiers and also served as a prison for captured American revolutionaries and their French allies. In 1783, Florida and the fort reverted to Spanish control as part of the Treaty of Paris which ended the American Revolution. After Spain ceded Florida to the United States in 1821, the Americans changed the name of the Castillo to Fort Marion in 1825. The fort was designated a national monument in 1924. In 1933, Fort Marion was transferred from the US War Department to the National Park Service and, in 1942, the fort's name was restored to Castillo de San Marcos.

FORT MATANZAS NATIONAL MONUMENT
8635 A1A South
904.471.0116
nps.gov/foma

The 1740 British siege of St. Augustine led by General James Oglethorpe convinced the Spanish that the southern approach to the city via the Matanzas River needed better protection. That year, the Spanish began construction of a coquina fortification to replace their wooden tower at Matanzas Inlet, about 15 miles south of St. Augustine. Informed of its construction by their Indian allies, the British made several unsuccessful attempts to destroy the fort. In 1741, two British warships were driven off by two Spanish vessels stationed at the inlet. In 1742, General Oglethorpe led a second expedition of a dozen British warships to St. Augustine but was repulsed by Spanish warships and batteries near St. Augustine Inlet. Believing Fort Matanzas to still be under construction, the British then tried to enter Matanzas Inlet. However, a warning shot fired from Fort Matanzas convinced the British that the fort was indeed completed and, with the approach of a storm, Oglethorpe abandoned the attempt and returned

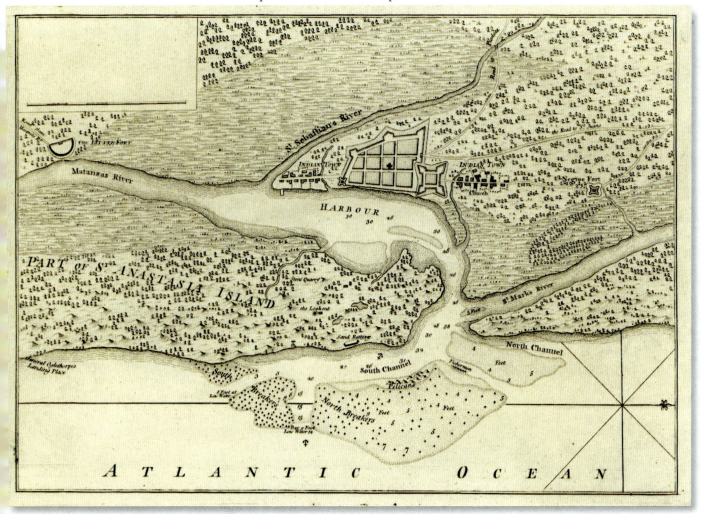

Plan of the town and harbor of St. Augustine by British cartographer Thomas Jefferys, 1763.
(Image courtesy of the Library of Congress)

Northeast Region

"Assault on Fort Mose" Battle of Fort Mose, June 1740.
(Artist: Jackson Walker, Image courtesy of the Florida National Guard)

to Georgia. In 1743, Oglethorpe again returned with several ships, but high seas prevented the British from entering the inlet or disembarking troops and the expedition was called off. During most of the British Period, the fort was maintained by a small garrison, sometimes as few as five British soldiers. By the end of the American Revolution, this number had increased to some 30 British regulars who improved its defenses in preparation for a possible attack from the Spanish who had entered the war against Great Britain. The fort was re-occupied by Spanish troops during the Second Spanish Period but little funding was available for its maintenance. By 1821, the fort had greatly deteriorated and, after the acquisition of Florida by the United States, it was never occupied by U.S. troops. The fort was designated a national monument in 1924. In 1933, responsibility for Fort Matanzas was transferred from the U.S. War Department to the National Park Service.

British King George III 1774 copper half-penny coin, found in Fernandina.
(Image courtesy of the Museum of Florida History)

Fort Mose Historic State Park
15 Fort Mose Trail
904.823.2232
floridastateparks.org/fortmose

In an effort to strike an economic blow to the English colonies to the north while at the same time adding settlers and Catholic converts to Florida, Spanish authorities promised religious sanctuary to runaway slaves from English colonies beginning in the late 1600s. In 1738, the Spanish established the fort and town of Gracia Real de Santa Teresa de Mose, or Fort Mose for short, as a sanctuary for escaped slaves. Located about two miles north of St. Augustine and manned by a free black company of Spanish militia, the fort offered protection to the city's northern approaches. During the British invasion of Florida led by General James Oglethorpe in 1740, the inhabitants of Fort Mose evacuated to the Castillo de San Marcos in St. Augustine. While the main British force laid siege to the Castillo, a force of about 140 British regulars, colonial militia and their Indian allies were detailed to occupy the abandoned fort. On June 26, 1740, a force of some 300 Spanish regulars, black militia and Indian allies launched a surprise attack from the Castillo against the British troops at Fort Mose. In the ensuing battle of "Bloody Mose," the British were defeated with losses of 68 dead and 34 captured. The Spanish, who suffered 10 killed, destroyed Fort Mose and returned to the Castillo with their prisoners. The following month, Oglethorpe called off the invasion and returned to Georgia.

Fort Mose was subsequently rebuilt by the Spanish in 1752 at

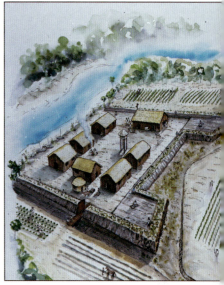
Artist rendering of Fort Mose.
(Image courtesy of the Fort Mose Historical Society)

Northeast Region

a new site slightly to the northeast of its original location. The fort was occupied by British troops in the first half of the British Period. However, with the onset of the American Revolution, the British determined that they did not have the manpower to garrison it and dismantled it in 1775. A military outpost was reestablished by the Spanish after they reacquired Florida in 1783 but, after driving out Americans who occupied the site during the Patriot War in 1812, the fort was destroyed for the last time by the Spanish. In 1989, the site of Fort Mose was purchased by the State of Florida, with additional acquisitions in 1998 and 2004. The park's visitor center and museum contains multimedia exhibits on the history of Fort Mose and artifacts recovered from the site. Interpretive panels are located throughout the park, including a State Historical Marker. The park is also host to annual living history events, including the "Flight To Freedom" program in February which reenacts the flight of escaped slaves from the British colonies to Fort Mose and the "Battle of Bloody Mose" reenactment held in June.

Government House
48 King Street
904.825.5034
staugustine.ufl.edu/govHouse.html

Throughout Florida's colonial periods, the Government House served as the governor's official residence and administrative office. The east wing of the present structure was constructed in c. 1710, during the First Spanish Period, to replace the governor's house destroyed during the English siege of 1702. During the British Period, the governors of East Florida resided there and ruled the colony from this building. During Governor James Grant's administration (1764-1771), the building was renovated with the installation of glazed double-hung sash widows, masonry fireplaces, and brick chimneys. A new kitchen, laundry, stable, and coach house were also added. Governor Grant was noted for the lavish parties he hosted at the house. Among the visitors to the Government House during this period was the famous frontiersman Daniel Boone who came to St. Augustine in 1765 to inquire about potential land purchases in East Florida. Following the American acquisition of Florida in 1821, the building underwent major renovations in 1833-1834, 1873, and 1936 which resulted in its present dimensions while retaining parts of its earlier walls. Owned by the State of Florida since 1966 and under the management of the University of Florida since 2010, the building now houses the Government House Museum. First-floor exhibits on the building's history include British Period artifacts uncovered during excavations on the property.

Horruytiner-Lindsley House
214 St. George Street

A plaque on this privately-owned house refers to it as the "Casa Horruytiner" and provides a brief summary of its history and architecture. Constructed during the First Spanish Period, the earliest documented owner of the house was a member of the prominent Spanish colonial Horruytiner family. During most of the British Period, it was owned by Dr. Robert Catherwood, a prominent British official who arrived in St. Augustine following the Spanish departure. In addition to being the civilian surgeon for British military forces in East Florida, he served as a member of the governing Council for East Florida from 1764 to 1783 and as a judge from 1776 to 1783. Catherwood also received land grants, including 20,000 acres on the western shore of the St. Johns River and 800 acres near Picolata, but these were apparently not developed. In 1783, he became embroiled in scandal when he was suspended from his offices on charges of speculating in captured slaves and extorting fees for justice. After the Spanish reacquired Florida, Catherwood left for the Bahamas in 1785 where he died the following year. The house subsequently passed through a succession of several owners until it was acquired by the Lindsley family in 1896 who owned it until 1977. This house is privately owned and is not open for tours.

The Governor's House at St. Augustine, 1764.
(Image courtesy of the British Library)

Northeast Region

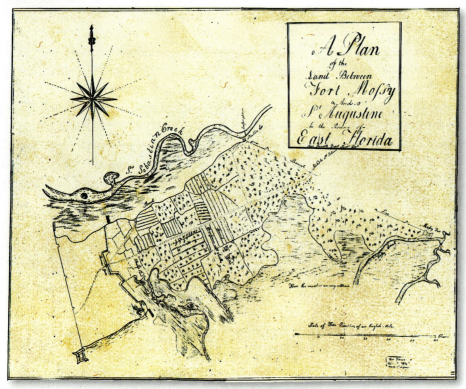
British Period map showing agricultural activities near St. Augustine.
(Image courtesy of the State Archives of Florida)

Oglethorpe Battery Park monument, Anastasia Island.
(Image courtesy of Frederick Gaske, Historic Preservation Consultant)

"King's Road" State Historical Marker
Palencia Club Drive

The text of this marker reads: "The British laid the original route for King's Road between 1772 and 1775 in an effort to encourage settlement into this area. Extending from St. Mary's, Georgia to Andrew Turnbull's Minorcan colony at New Smyrna, King's Road intersects Palencia Club Drive at this point. The initial construction of King's Road included bridges for crossing creeks & wetlands. When the American Colonies declared independence from England in 1776, nearly 7,000 Loyalists used this route to seek asylum in Florida, which remained loyal to the British Crown. When the British left Florida as part of the 1783 Treaty of Paris ending the Revolutionary War, maintenance of King's Road lagged until Florida became a U.S. territory in 1821. During the early 20th century, oyster shell was added to the road bed & some areas were paved with red brick. Portions of the original course of King's Road have been incorporated into modern trails and roads, particularly US 1, or are abandoned such as the portion visible here."

Oglethorpe Battery Park
Oglethorpe Boulevard and Arredondo Avenue

A small park on Anastasia Island maintained by the City of St. Augustine is located in the area from which the British bombarded the Castillo de San Marcos during their siege of the city in 1740. On March 20, 1938, an approximately 20-foot tall coquina obelisk monument commemorating this event was dedicated at the site by the monument's sponsor, the St. Augustine Historical Society and Institute of Science. The dedication ceremony was attended by hundreds of spectators, including representatives of three states – Florida, Georgia, and South Carolina - whose soldiers participated in the engagement. Known as the Oglethorpe Monument, the monument's pedestal contains bronze tablets with historical and sponsorship information on all four sides. A State Historical Marker for the "Oglethorpe Battery Park" is also located in the park, the text of which reads: "From this site, General James Oglethorpe, commanding military forces from Georgia and Carolina, bombarded Castillo de San Marcos from June 27 to July 20, 1740. The Castillo's massive coquina walls absorbed the cannon shot and damage was slight. Florida's Spanish Governor, Manuel de Montiano, returned the fire, but the exchange was indecisive. Provisions arrived from Havana just in time to relieve a critical shortage which

General James Oglethorpe.
(Image courtesy of the State Archives of Florida)

NORTHEAST REGION

would have caused St. Augustine to capitulate. Frustrated by the military stalemate and the oncoming hurricane season, Oglethorpe withdrew to Georgia." In 2013, three replica cannons mounted on masonry carriages were installed in the park to commemorate the 1740 siege. The cannons were sponsored by the Ancient City Chapter of the Military Officers Association of America in cooperation with several other civic organizations. A flag pole for the British Red Ensign flag was also erected at the park in 2013 by the St. Augustine British Club and other sponsors.

OLDEST HOUSE MUSEUM COMPLEX
14 St. Francis Street
904.824.2872
staugustinehistoricalsociety.org/old-house.html

Owned and operated by the St. Augustine Historical Society, the museum complex includes the Gonzalez-Alvarez House which was constructed in the early 1700s during the First Spanish Period. After the British acquisition of Florida in 1763, this house, along with many others in St. Augustine, passed to the control of Jesse Fish, who had come to Florida in the 1730s as the representative of William Walton's New York mercantile firm. Under the terms of the 1763 Treaty of Paris, the departing Spanish were allowed an 18 month period to sell their property to British subjects, but there were few buyers. Rather than risk the forfeiture of their properties to the British Crown, many Spanish owners of unsold lots and buildings in the city transferred them to Fish in the hope that he could sell them as the market improved and forward the proceeds to them in their new homes in Cuba. By some estimates, Fish controlled more than one-half of all the private homes in the city. On nearby Anastasia Island, Fish purchased 10,000 acres and established a citrus plantation named El Vergel (The Orchard). Fish remained in Florida during the Second Spanish Period and was buried on his plantation upon his death in 1790.

In 1775, Fish sold the Gonzalez-Alvarez House to Sergeant Major Joseph Peavett, the acting paymaster for the British troops, and his wife Mary Evans, a midwife. Peavett eventually acquired over 2,000 acres of land in East Florida which he farmed with the use of enslaved Africans and also served as a member of the East Florida Assembly. The story of his wife Mary's life in St. Augustine became the subject of a popular 1977 novel, *Maria*, by the best-selling author Eugenia Price. During the Peavett ownership, the house was enlarged with the

Map of St. Augustine by John de Solis, 1764.
(Image courtesy of the State Archives of Florida)

Jesse Fish and Land Speculation in British St. Augustine

In the hectic days preceding the arrival of British troops at St. Augustine in 1763, desperate Spaniards were unable to sell their houses and lots. Jesse Fish, an English colonial who had resided in the Spanish town for decades and had become a friend of the local Spaniards, reached an agreement with them only weeks before their departure. Fish accepted deeds to their properties--nearly half the housing stock in the town--as payment for the debts they owed to his employer, William Walton and Company of New York. Fish assumed the debts with the understanding that he would pay them off as the properties were sold to incoming British settlers. He promised to send the excess proceeds, minus fees and a commission for himself, to the former owners in Havana. It was a deal that went bad for Fish, and according to some journalists and historians who have vilified him through the years, bad for the Spaniards who signed over their properties. Whether or not Fish kept his promise is still debated.

Soon after the Spaniards departed St. Augustine, British soldiers burned some of the houses and vandalized others, greatly reducing their resale values. When William Walton terminated his business in St. Augustine, Jesse Fish was out of a job but still deeply in debt to his former employer for the debts he had assumed, and interest charges continued to mount. Eventually, the properties were sold, but critics charge that Fish failed to transmit all of the proceeds and charged excessive fees. Fish insisted that he acted honestly and charitably and that he in fact suffered great financial losses for his efforts. To further complicate matters, he was apparently the victim of embezzlement by friends and relatives who betrayed his trust. Through the intervention of Luciano de Herrera, one of three Spanish men who remained in St. Augustine under the British, the confusion was untangled and funds were transmitted to Havana to satisfy most of the former owners. Fish remained mired in debt until the end of his life.

NORTHEAST REGION

addition of the second story and other improvements were made. Like Fish, Peavett remained in St. Augustine after the Spanish reacquired Florida and died in 1786. House owners began promoting it as the city's "Oldest House" and a tourist attraction in the late 1800s and, in 1918, it was purchased by the St. Augustine Historical Society for use as a house museum. Also located in the museum complex is the Manucy Museum in the 1924 Webb Building. This museum contains exhibits on local and regional history, including a British Period exhibit with artifacts.

PENA-PECK HOUSE
143 St. George Street
904.829.5064
penapeckhouse.com

The Pena-Peck House was constructed in ca. 1750 of native coquina stone as the residence of Juan Estaban de Pena, the Spanish Royal Treasurer in St. Augustine from 1742 to 1763. During the British Period, glazed sash widows and brick chimneys were added and it was enlarged with a third wing to form a U-shaped building around a garden. From 1772 to 1778, it was the in-town home of John Moultrie, the lieutenant

East Florida Lieutenant Governor John Moultrie.
(Image courtesy of the State Archives of Florida)

Pena-Peck House, St. Augustine.
(Image courtesy of photographer Hookey Hamilton, St. Augustine)

governor of East Florida from 1767 until he left for England in 1784. Moultrie also served as the Acting Governor of the province from 1771 to 1774. Moultrie was granted large tracts of land in the St. Augustine vicinity, including the 2,000-acre Rosetta Plantation on the Tomoka River and the 2,500-acre Bella Vista Plantation on the Matanzas River where he spent much of his time. At Bella Vista, Moultrie constructed a grandiose Georgian-Palladian style mansion, considered by many as the grandest country estate in East Florida. The Spanish regained control of Florida in 1783, but the British did not complete their evacuation until 1785. In the period between the arrival of the new Spanish governor in 1784 and the British departure, the British Governor of East Florida, Patrick Tonyn, moved his offices from the Government House to the Pena-Peck House, in essence making it the last seat of British government in East Florida. After a series of owners and renters, the house was purchased in 1837 by Dr. Seth Peck, who added a second story made of wood. The house was donated to the City of St. Augustine in 1931 by Peck's granddaughter, Anna Gardner Burt. Since 1932, it has been managed and exhibited as a house museum by the Woman's Exchange of St. Augustine, a non-profit service organization. The visitor's orientation room contains panels on the building's history including one on "Life During the British Period." An exhibit case in the room contains British Period artifacts recovered during excavations at the house.

"PRISONERS OF WAR IN ST. AUGUSTINE DURING THE AMERICAN REVOLUTION" HISTORICAL MARKER
King Street and St. George Street

The text of this marker reads: "From the onset of the American Revolution in 1775, the British Crown Colony in East Florida was a Loyalist bastion. In its capital, St. Augustine, the British lodged as prisoners many American Patriots and their French allies. Most of these prisoners were given the liberty of the town, but some were held in Castillo de San Marcos. A few captives rented quarters, but most of the men were housed in the unfinished State House which stood near this spot. By the end of 1780, these prisoners included three signers of the Declaration of Independence--Thomas Heyward, Jr., Arthur Middleton, and Edward Rutledge. On July 4, 1781, the Patriot captives celebrated Independence Day." This marker was erected in 1996 by the Florida State Society of the Daughters of the American Revolution.

Northeast Region

"Wrath of the Privateers" Sir Francis Drake's raid on St. Augustine, 1586.
(Artist: Jackson Walker, Image courtesy of the Legendary Florida Collection)

St. Augustine Art Association
22 Marine Street
904.824.2310
staaa.org

In 1585-1586, an English fleet of 29 ships with over 2,000 men, under the command of Sir Francis Drake, conducted an expedition against Spanish colonies in the West Indies. After attacking Spanish cities in the Caribbean and capturing numerous ships, the now expanded fleet of 42 ships headed north along the coast of Spanish Florida and raided St. Augustine. The greatly outnumbered Spanish were forced to flee inland until after the raid. Drake's men set fire to the city's buildings, wrecked crops, and seized or destroyed anything of value. A permanent exhibit in the St. Augustine Art Association building displays items dating to Drake's 1586 attack on St. Augustine. The artifacts were uncovered during a 1998 excavation conducted by the St. Augustine City Archaeologist prior to the construction of a new wing on the Art Association building. A burn layer from a building destroyed in the 1586 raid was uncovered and the associated artifacts include Spanish and Native American pottery, a stitching needle, and a building spike. A living history reenactment of "Drake's Raid" is held annually in St. Augustine in June.

St. Augustine Historical Society Research Library
12 Aviles Street
904.825.2333
staugustinehistoricalsociety.org/library.html

In addition to the Oldest House Museum Complex, the St. Augustine Historical Society maintains a research library in the Segui-Kirby Smith House which was constructed in the late 1700s. Focusing primarily on St. Augustine and St. Johns County, the extensive resources include books, microfilm, maps, photographs, newspapers, manuscripts, and other records. Among the items in the microfilm collection are the records of the British Colonial Office, the governmental department responsible for administering colonial possessions, for British East Florida. The library also contains an extensive collection of genealogical data, particularly for descendants of the Minorcans who first came to Florida during the British Period.

St. Augustine Lighthouse and Museum
81 Lighthouse Avenue
904.825.2333
staugustinelighthouse.org

The existing brick St. Augustine Lighthouse was constructed in 1874 to replace an earlier coquina lighthouse threatened by erosion, becoming the latest in a series of watchtowers and lighthouses at this site dating back to the First Spanish Period. During the British Period,

NORTHEAST REGION

a coquina watch tower originally constructed by the Spanish was raised some 60 feet with a wooden framework and a cannon was placed on top to signal the approach of a vessel. The tower was regularly referred to as a lighthouse or beacon in British charts and maps of the period. After the American acquisition of Florida, the colonial tower was converted into the new territory's first official lighthouse in 1824. Located about 500 yards northeast of the present lighthouse, it collapsed in 1880. A State Historical Marker for "Sentinels of the Coast" is located near its site.

The Lighthouse Archaeological Maritime Program (LAMP), the research division of the St. Augustine Lighthouse and Museum, conducts underwater archaeological work in St. Johns County. Since the late 1990s, Lighthouse archaeologists have been involved in excavating and monitoring the remains of the British sloop *Industry* which was carrying supplies for the British army garrison in St. Augustine when it wrecked on a sandbar off the city in 1764. Numerous artifacts from the ship's cargo of military supplies and tools have been excavated and conserved. Many of the recovered artifacts are on display in the restored 1876 Lighthouse Keeper's House, including a cannon and a swivel gun. In 2009, LAMP archaeologists discovered a shipwreck, known as the "Storm Wreck," which appears to be the remains of a British ship that was carrying Loyalist refugees from Charleston, South Carolina to St. Augustine and wrecked on a sandbar off the city on December 31, 1782. Recovered artifacts, including a rare carronade (short cast iron cannon), the ship's bell, a flintlock pistol, and a British army uniform button, are in the process of being conserved for future display. Guests can visit the laboratory and see the artifacts on a "Behind the Scenes Tour" or "The Lost Ships Archaeo Tour." Another LAMP project involves the search for the *Dove*, a British slave ship which wrecked on the St. Augustine bar in 1773. Also at the lighthouse is a small craft boatworks, a traditional wooden boatbuilding program which constructs replicas of vessels once common in St. Augustine waters. One project involves the construction of a 14-foot British yawl (a ship's boat carried on a larger sailing vessel) based on a 1760 Royal Navy design.

Map of 1586 Drake attack on St. Augustine by Baptista Boazio, 1589.
(Image courtesy of the State Archives of Florida)

Sir Francis Drake and the 1586 English Raid on St. Augustine

From 1565, when Admiral Pedro Menéndez de Avilés established Spain's La Florida colony at St. Augustine, until 1763, when the colony was ceded to the British, the soldiers and colonists faced hurricanes, attacks by Native Americans, food shortages, murderous and destructive attacks by English buccaneers, and invasions by British colonials from South Carolina and Georgia. Recurring epidemic diseases like smallpox, yellow fever, and measles resulted in death for many thousands of Native Americans at Franciscan missions throughout the colony. Rebellions at the missions brought further death and destruction. La Florida was, as the scholar Dr. Amy Bushnell has written, for many decades a "land of living war." Two attacks on St. Augustine, by Sir Francis Drake in 1586 and by Captain Robert Searles in 1668, left alarming British trails in Florida.

The attack led by Sir Francis Drake came in 1586 and ended a brief period of peace for the beleaguered residents of the Spanish province. Drake and 2,000 men aboard 42 vessels were returning to England after attacking and plundering Cartagena when they seized an opportunity to plunder another Spanish settlement. The Spanish soldiers and civilians fled from the town with the few possessions they could carry. Drake's men, joined by Indians, looted and torched the houses and destroyed the groves and gardens. In the months that followed, Spanish officials decided to evacuate Santa Elena (today at Parris Island, South Carolina), the town founded by Pedro Menéndez as his home and the first capital of Florida. Residents of Santa Elena were moved to St. Augustine, which then became the capital.

NORTHEAST REGION

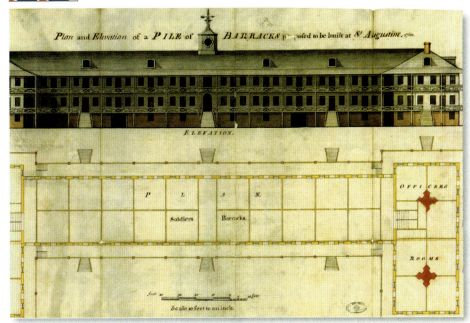

Plan for British barracks at St. Augustine, 1768.
(Image courtesy of the National Archives of the United Kingdom)

ST. FRANCIS BARRACKS AND THE KING'S BAKERY
82 Marine Street and 97 Marine Street
904.823.0364
floridaguard.army.mil

Portions of the St. Francis Barracks building were originally constructed by the Spanish of coquina in the early to mid-1700s for use as a Catholic Franciscan monastery and church. After the British acquired Florida, the Spanish monastery and church were converted into military barracks for British troops stationed in St. Augustine. An extensive renovation of the complex for this purpose was completed in 1771. The British also constructed a huge wooden barracks south of the St. Francis Barracks. Known as the Pile of Barracks, the wooden structure was prefabricated in New York and shipped to St. Augustine to be erected on a brick and stone foundation. Under supervision of a royal engineer, Colonel James Moncrief, the three-story structure was constructed between September 1770 and August 1771. Across the street from the two British barracks, facing west on today's Marine Street, a coquina structure was erected for use as a bakery to supply bread for the soldiers. During the Second Spanish Period, the buildings continued in use as a military installation for the Spanish garrison, although the wooden barracks were destroyed by fire in 1792. After the American acquisition of Florida, the St. Francis Barracks remained in military usage and during the Civil War housed first Confederate troops and then Union units. Now the headquarters of the Florida National Guard, the Barracks contains a small museum, which is open by appointment, on the military history of Florida. The King's Bakery building, located in the National Guard military compound, is the only extant building entirely constructed during the British Period in St. Augustine.

TOLOMATO CEMETERY
14 Cordova Street
tolomatocemetery.com

During the First Spanish Period, this site was part of a Franciscan mission which included a village of Christianized Indians. After the 1763 British acquisition of Florida, these Indians and their Spanish friars departed for Cuba. In 1777, the indentured Italian, Greek, and Minorcan laborers from Andrew Turnbull's Smyrnea Settlement at today's New Smyrna Beach and Edgewater fled to St. Augustine en masse claiming mistreatment by Turnbull and his overseers. Their Catholic pastor, Father Pedro Camps, came with them and received permission from British East Florida Governor Patrick Tonyn to use a portion of the old mission site as a cemetery for his parishioners. The cemetery continued in use as a Catholic burial ground until its closure in 1884.

Among those buried here is Francisco Xavier Sanchez who died in 1807. Born in St. Augustine in 1736, Sanchez managed the San Diego Plantation, the original family homestead which had been granted to his father north of St. Augustine, during the First Spanish Period. One of the few Spanish residents to stay in Florida after its acquisition by the British, his landholdings eventually stretched for thousands of acres along the Diego Plains from the St. Johns River to near the St. Marys River. He acquired over 1,000 acres from the British Crown and thousands more during the Second Spanish Period. Operated by enslaved African labor, his plantations produced a wide variety of agricultural products, raised large herds of cattle, and harvested hardwoods and other timber products. Sanchez also operated mercantile and shipping interests, and he owned a number of properties in St. Augustine. During the American Revolution, Sanchez provided food and clothing to Spanish, French, and American prisoners of war held by the British in St. Augustine, including three signers of the Declaration of Independence. In 2013, the Florida Society of the Sons of the American Revolution dedicated a plaque to Sanchez at Tolomato Cemetery for his "patriotic service during the American Revolution."

Northeast Region

Tovar House
22 St. Francis Street
904.824.2872

Constructed in the mid-1700s during the First Spanish Period, the Tovar House was left in the care of Jesse Fish when its owner left St. Augustine at the beginning of the British Period. In 1768, Fish sold the house to John Johnson, a Scottish merchant who owned a pub and inn in St. Augustine. During his occupancy, Johnson made no changes to the size of the house. In 1782, St. Johns Town was established at what is known today as St. Johns Bluff in Duval County. Located on the St. Johns River only six miles from the Atlantic Ocean, St. Johns Town quickly became the second most populous town in British East Florida following an influx of British Loyalist refugees from Charleston and Savannah. At St. Johns Town, Johnson established a mercantile operation in partnership with John Michel who lived in the community. Following the Spanish reacquisition of Florida in 1783, Johnson presumably vacated St. Augustine as the 1788 Mariano de la Rocque map of the city shows the property to be in the possession

British St. Augustine and East Florida's Governors

In 1763, Britain's East Florida colony extended westward from the Atlantic Ocean to the Apalachicola River but contained only one town, St. Augustine. When British troops first arrived at St. Augustine, the entire Spanish population, with the exception of three families, was preparing to depart. Soldiers familiar with London were shocked by how small the town was. The town extended from north to south for nearly one mile, but was only about a quarter of a mile deep.

Only 300 houses were standing in the town, mostly one-story structures made of coquina stone, tabby or wood. One block north of the central plaza, stood the most impressive structure found anywhere in East or West Florida, the Castillo de San Marcos, whose sturdy coquina stone walls had twice withstood British siege and bombardment.

Three men, two born in Scotland, the third born in South Carolina of Scot parents, governed British East Florida. The first governor, Colonel James Grant, was born at Ballindalloch in the Highlands of Scotland. He was appointed governor in 1763 after serving in the British army in North America and the Caribbean during the Seven Years' War. Grant's tenure in office was noteworthy for his successful negotiation of peace treaties with the Creek and Seminole Indians of the region, and for his successful promotion of plantation development and export agriculture. Grant advocated labor systems resembling the plantations of Georgia, South Carolina, and Caribbean colonies, where the work was done by enslaved Africans rather than indentured Europeans. To set an example, Grant established an indigo plantation worked by slave laborers that became the most profitable estate in the province.

In St. Augustine, the bon vivant bachelor governor was famous for his lavish dinner parties and liberal dispensation of wine, rum, and brandy. Grant's meals were prepared by Baptiste, an enslaved African who had been trained as a chef in Paris. It may have been the gourmet meals and abundant libations that necessitated Grant's return to London for medical treatment in 1771.

During Grant's absence, which was intended to be temporary, John Moultrie served as interim governor. Moultrie, born into a wealthy South Carolina family, was a physician trained at Edinburgh University in Scotland and a highly successful planter and slave owner. He brought his slaves from Carolina to East Florida and developed several profitable indigo, rice, and cotton plantations south of St. Augustine. Moultrie is also remembered for supervising an ambitious public works program that resulted in the construction of government buildings in St. Augustine and the Kings Road that connected the capital to the plantations south along the Atlantic Coast, and ran north to the Georgia border. After a permanent governor was named to replace Grant, who resigned in April 1773 to take a seat in Parliament, Moultrie served as lieutenant governor.

Patrick Tonyn, from Northumberland County in Scotland, was appointed the second governor of British East Florida in 1774. An army officer, Patrick Tonyn served with distinction in Germany during the Seven Years' War. The owner of a 20,000-acre plantation at Black Creek and St. Johns River, Tonyn had barely settled into his St. Augustine quarters before the American Revolution broke out. He adeptly negotiated a treaty of alliance with the Seminole and Creek that paid handsome dividends when rebels from Georgia invaded East Florida. An argumentative man, Tonyn alienated several of East Florida's most important planters, who abandoned the province. He was, however, a successful wartime governor who strengthened provincial defenses and organized an effective colonial militia, the East Florida Rangers.

East Florida's first governor, James Grant.
(Image courtesy of the State Archives of Florida)

East Florida's second governor, Patrick Tonyn.
(Image courtesy of the State Archives of Florida)

Northeast Region

of the King of Spain. Following a series of private owners, the house was acquired by the St. Augustine Historical Society in 1918. Today, the Tovar House is operated by the Society as part of its Oldest House Museum complex. During a 1880s renovation, two cannonballs were reported as being found embedded in the east wall of the house and attributed to the 1740 British siege of St. Augustine. It is now believed they were inserted at a much later date.

Southern St. Johns County

"Double Bridges and the Old King's Road 1772" State Historical Marker

Dark Horse Lane near Pellicer Creek (In gated community)

The text of this marker reads: "The King's Road, an overland highway constructed during Florida's British Colonial period (1763-1784), once traversed the Double Bridges property at this location. The road spanned Pellicer Creek, Hulett Branch, and swamp wetlands over a system of wooden bridges and raised earthen causeways. This crossing has long been called Double Bridges, named for the unusual combination of the two spans built so close together. Remnants of the King's Road, marked by road cuts through high sandy bluffs and a short section of a causeway, are visible here. A longer section of causeway can be seen on the south side of Pellicer Creek. The bridges are gone, but remaining piers and extensive earthworks serve as monuments to this historic crossing. The causeways and bridges, spanning some 625 feet of swampland, were once an important part of the 18th century road that connected St. Augustine and New Smyrna. This major project, commissioned in 1772, was built to solidify East Florida as the British Crown's 14th colony. Double Bridges and the Old King's Road were recorded to the Florida Master Site File as historic sites 8SJ4892 and 8SJ4893 in 2002."

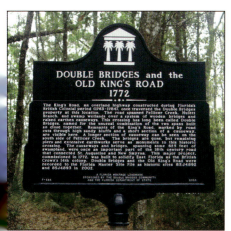

Double Bridges and the Old King's Road State Historical Marker.
(Image courtesy of Vale Fillmon, Florida State Historical Marker Program)

Rebel Prisoners in Loyal St. Augustine

During the American Revolution, 63 prisoners of war, all prominent rebels captured when Charleston fell to British arms in May 1780, were transported to St. Augustine. Three of the prisoners, Thomas Heyward Jr., Arthur Middleton, and Edward Rutledge, had signed the Declaration of Independence. The group also included Christopher Gadsden, who was a leader of the Sons of Liberty and attended the First Continental Congress as an elected delegate in July 1774. Still determined to resist British authority, Gadsden scorned Governor Tonyn's offer of parole and remained a prisoner in Fort St. Mark.

It may have been the meager rations and the damp and cold of the fort that convinced the others to accept conditions of parole that included a promise to not attempt escape. Confident "these incendiaries can do little mischief here," Tonyn warned residents of the town to avoid "friendly intercourse" with the prisoners or risk the displeasure of the governor.

Josiah Smith, Jr. chronicled the experiences of his comrades after being paroled, noting that Alexander Moultrie and family moved to the Bella Vista, the country residence of his older brother, Lt. Governor John Moultrie. The wealthy among the parolees formed three "mess groups" and moved into comfortable rented homes, joined by their servants. The less wealthy parolees slept in meager rented rooms or spare rooms in the State House. The prisoners reported to the State House twice a day and placed red badges around the necks of servants.

American patriot Christopher Gadsden.
(Image courtesy of the Library of Congress)

In July 1781, the rebels were placed aboard four ships bound for Charleston and Philadelphia. St. Augustine residents Jesse Fish and Francisco Sanchez, merchants looking ahead to a time when commerce with the newly formed United States of America would begin, stocked the departing boats with provisions.

Christopher Gadsden was transported to Philadelphia. He later wrote to General George Washington to describe his 42 week confinement: forbidden in the early months to receive visitors and denied candles at night, his jailors eventually relented and in general "behaved with decency." Ever the fiery revolutionary, Gadsden told Washington that he refused parole to be seen as his "Standing protest" against tyranny.

NORTHEAST REGION

Francis Philip Fatio
(Image courtesy of the State Archives of Florida)

Switzerland

"NEW SWITZERLAND PLANTATION" HISTORICAL MARKER
State Road 13 near Swiss Road

Born in Switzerland in 1724, Francis Philip Fatio moved in 1771 from London to East Florida where he and several business partners obtained large land grants from the British authorities. The largest grant consisted of 10,000 acres with twelve miles of riverfront on the east side of the St. Johns River, which was named New Switzerland in honor of the country of Fatio's birth. Fatio eventually purchased his partners' interests and became sole owner of the plantation. Operated by enslaved labor, Fatio initially grew indigo and rice on the plantation, but successfully diversified to the production of timber, naval stores such as turpentine, citrus, cattle, cotton, corn, and other crops. During the American Revolution, Fatio became a British army officer and was stationed in Charleston. Unlike most of his fellow British countrymen who left Florida after it was ceded back to Spain in 1783, Fatio remained and continued to prosper during the Second Spanish Period until he died in 1811. In 1812, the New Switzerland plantation buildings were burned and destroyed by Georgia militia during the invasion of East Florida known as the Patriot War. A historical marker for the "New Switzerland Plantation" was erected by the St. Johns County Historical Commission in 1997 in the vicinity of Fatio's plantation.

WESTERN ST. JOHNS COUNTY

"WILLIAM BARTRAM'S PLANTATION" STATE HISTORICAL MARKER
State Road 16 at Shands Bridge east of the St. Johns River

The text of this marker reads: "In 1766 on the banks of the St. Johns River at Little Florence Cove, William Bartram attempted to farm a 500-acre land grant. Bartram had spent much of the previous year exploring the new British colony of East Florida with his father, John Bartram, the Royal Botanist for America under King George III. When John Bartram returned home, near Philadelphia, the younger Bartram stayed in Florida. He hoped like many other settlers to make a fortune exporting cash crops such as indigo and rice. Using six enslaved Africans, Bartram cleared the forest and planted, but within a year he abandoned his farm and returned home. Bartram was known in England for illustrating his father's botanical specimens. Between 1773-1777 patrons financed Bartram's further exploration of the American Southeast. In 1791, he published his observations in *Travels Through North and South Carolina, Georgia, East and West Florida*, one of the most influential travel accounts of the American frontier. Rather than write a mere scientific catalog, Bartram produced a joyful and tender portrait of a virgin land 'with an infinite variety of animated scenes, inexpressibly beautiful and pleasing' which inspired the poets of England's Romantic Movement."

WILLIAM BARTRAM SCENIC AND HISTORIC HIGHWAY
State Road 13 between Julington Creek Bridge and State Road 16

In 1980, the Florida Legislature designated a 17.3 mile portion of State Road 13 which runs parallel to the St. Johns River in St. Johns County as the "William Bartram Scenic Highway" in honor of the naturalist who traveled through this area during the British Period. A historical marker for the "William Bartram Scenic Highway" was erected on State Road 13 near Swamp Oak Trail. Erected by the Arvida/St Joe Company, this marker provides information on the Native American history of the area. In 2005, the renamed "William Bartram Scenic & Historic Highway" was designated as a Florida Scenic Highway.

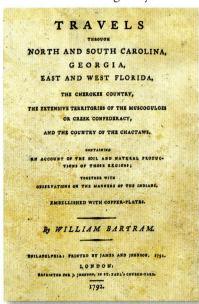

Title page of William Bartram's book *Travels*.
(Image courtesy of the State Archives of Florida)

CENTRAL REGION

BREVARD COUNTY

Cocoa

THE FLORIDA HISTORICAL SOCIETY
435 Brevard Avenue
321.690.1971
myfloridahistory.org

Founded in 1856 in St. Augustine, the primary mission of the Florida Historical Society is to collect, preserve, and publish materials relating to the history of Florida and its peoples. After a period of inactivity beginning during the Civil War, it resumed operation in 1902. The society publishes the *Florida Historical Quarterly* and maintains the Library of Florida History, an extensive collection of historical documents, maps, and photographs, in the restored 1939 Old Cocoa Federal Building. The collection contains documents relating to the British in Florida, including a 1776 Bernard Romans' "General Map of the Southern British Colonies in America" and papers of the Panton, Leslie & Company which dominated the Indian trade in British East Florida, and in West Florida during the Second Spanish Period.

Battle of the USS *Alliance* and HMS *Sybil*, last naval battle of the American Revolution, off the coast of Cape Canaveral, Florida on March 10, 1783.
(Image courtesy of the Naval History and Heritage Command, U.S. Department of the Navy)

Merritt Island

"LAST NAVAL BATTLE OF THE AMERICAN REVOLUTIONARY WAR" STATE HISTORICAL MARKER
Veterans Memorial Park
400 South Sykes Creek Parkway

The text of this marker reads: "The last naval battle of the American Revolutionary War took place off the coast of Cape Canaveral on March 10, 1783. The fight began when three British ships sighted two Continental Navy ships, the *Alliance* commanded by Captain John Barry and the *Duc De Lauzun* commanded by Captain John Green sailing northward along the coast of Florida. The *Alliance*, a 36-gun frigate, and the *Duc De Lauzun*, a 20-gun ship, were loaded with 72,000 Spanish silver dollars they were bringing from Havana, Cuba to Philadelphia to support the Continental Army. One of the British ships, the HMS *Sybil*, a 28-gun frigate, commanded

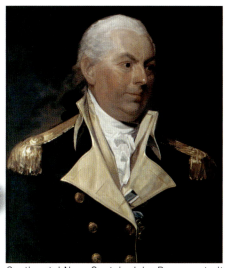
Continental Navy Captain John Barry, portrait by Gilbert Stuart, 1801.
(Image courtesy of the Naval History and Heritage Command, U.S. Department of the Navy)

Pewter bowl and spoon recovered from a British ship that wrecked off St. Augustine in 1782.
(Image courtesy of the St. Augustine Lighthouse and Museum)

CENTRAL REGION

by Captain James Vashon, chased the *Alliance* and *Duc De Lauzun* to the south. The HMS *Sybil* fired first, exchanging shots with the slower *Duc De Lauzun*. Then in a daring strategy Captain John Barry aboard the *Alliance* reversed his course, and while under fire, waited until the HMS *Sybil* was close. When the British ship was alongside he returned fire to the broadside with greater number of cannon. The battle lasted less than an hour, when the HMS *Sybil*, outgunned and badly damaged, broke off from the battle and fled. The *Alliance* and *Duc De Lauzun* then continued on their mission at dawn on March 11, 1783."

Following the Revolutionary War, John Barry earned the sobriquet "The Father of the American Navy" for his role in commanding and developing the nascent U.S. Navy after its creation in 1794. In front of the State Historical Marker is a modern cast of a Revolutionary War period cannon mounted on a masonry carriage. Dedicated in 2007 at Cape Canaveral on the 224th anniversary of the battle, the marker was moved to its current location in 2011.

LAKE COUNTY
Fruitland Park

Holy Trinity Episcopal Church
2201 Spring Lake Road
352.787.1500
holytrinityfp.com

This church is the only remaining structure associated with a 1880s British settlement known as the Chetwynd Colony. Induced by advertisements in English newspapers with promises of cheap land, groups of British settlers came to Central Florida in the late 19th century to seek their fortunes in the citrus industry. One such settlement was established in 1882 near Fruitland Park by Granville Chetwynd Stapylton, a British entrepreneur who also erected a complex at the settlement for boarding and instructing his fellow Englishmen on citrus cultivation. Stapylton also purchased the property on which the Holy Trinity Episcopal Church was constructed in 1888 in the Carpenter Gothic style. The Great Freezes of 1894-1895 and 1899 destroyed much of the region's citrus crop and the Chetwynd Colony was abandoned shortly after. While the other settlement buildings have since been demolished, the church remains as the only remnant of this short-lived British colony. A State Historical Marker erected at the church in 1976 provides information on its history.

Florida Pine Forests Become a Mainstay of the British Economy

During the American War of Independence, ships sailing between Florida and Britain were subject to attack and confiscation by enemy navies and privateers. With access to British markets blocked, planters in East and West Florida could no longer rely on sales of indigo dye for income. Planters in the rebel colonies of New England and the Carolinas were confronted with a similar dilemma when they were unable to sell forest products, provisions, and salt fish in the British Caribbean colonies. West Florida residents, with access to what seemed an endless supply of fish from the Gulf of Mexico and huge forest reserves, found ready markets in Jamaica and other West Indies colonies. In East Florida, with its vast stands of pine forests, exports of timber and naval stores for the Royal Navy--tar, pitch, and turpentine--soon replaced indigo dye as the main source of income.

This economic transformation was most apparent along the St. Johns River and other waterways in East Florida. At Francis Levett's 10,000-acre Julianton Plantation, enslaved workers slashed 150,000 pine trees with the recognizable V scars and attached boxes with buckets to catch the flow of pine sap that was distilled for turpentine. Denys Rolle, Member of Parliament and a mostly absentee planter in East Florida, had 30,000 pine trees slashed and boxed at his 3,000-acre Chichester Plantation, one of several he owned on the St. Johns River.

Near the entrance to the St. Johns River, numerous properties were converted to naval stores production, and wharves and storehouses sprang up along the shore and on several of the islands. William Panton and Thomas Forbes became leaders in the turpentine trade. Known primarily as Indian traders after they purchased the Florida trade stores of the James Spalding and Roger Kelsall firm, Panton and Forbes invested heavily in naval stores trade operations centered on 3,000 acres in the vicinity of Forbes Bluff (today known as Fulton in Jacksonville) and the Lower St. Johns River basin. They also purchased Turpentine Island, closer to the river entrance. At the bluff, the storehouses and wharves accommodated thousands of barrels of tar, pitch, and turpentine each year.

Naval stores production using enslaved labor.
(Image courtesy of the University of North Carolina Library)

Shoe buckle from a 1782 British shipwreck site.
(Image courtesy of St. Augustine Lighthouse and Museum)

CENTRAL REGION

ORANGE COUNTY
Conway

"THE ENGLISH COLONY" HISTORICAL MARKER
Conway Road and Lake Margaret Drive

Erected in 2009 by Orange County, the text of this marker reads:

"A group of Englishmen known locally as the English Colony immigrated to Conway in the 1880s. They came as a result of a land and citrus industry promotion by the state and railroad corporations that promised an annual income of at least $10,000 growing oranges. These settlers were a mixed group of older retired professional men and army officers, a younger group who was supported by family in England, and laborers who came as servants. The Englishmen planted their orange groves but were not businessmen as much as they were sports enthusiasts. They spent their leisure time playing tennis, riding bicycles on the hard-packed roads, and shooting large flocks of pigeons as they flew to the abundant lakes for water. The group formed a yacht club on Lake Conway

An 1880s British Mini-Invasion of Florida

One century after Britain ceded East Florida to Spain, a new wave of immigrants from England settled in central Florida. They intended to plant orange, lemon, lime and grapefruit trees and prosper from sales of fruit from their groves.

In 1880, nearly all of Florida's 250,000 residents were located in the northern part of the state. Efforts to promote settlement further south had been stymied by impoverished state finances and primitive transportation facilities.

To break this deadlock, Governor William D. Bloxham agreed in 1881 to sell four million acres of public land to Philadelphia industrialist Hamilton Disston for a cash payment of $1 million. Disston also contracted to drain nine million acres of swamp and overflowed land in return for title to one-half of the land he drained. Dredges were soon at work digging canals, and farmers followed to establish homesteads on the drained land. Disston's agents aggressively sold the land in northern U.S. and European cities.

Additional millions of acres of public land were granted to railroad companies owned by Henry Plant and Henry M. Flagler. With Plant and Flagler organizing land sales companies, settlers began moving near the rail lines and shipping produce to northern cities.

In 1882 English investor Sir Edward Reed paid $600,000 to Disston for two million acres of land. Reed's Florida Land and Mortgage Company of London placed ads in *The Times* of London touting Florida as the "Italy of America" where the "second sons" of wealthy families could prosper. One result was the "English Colony" at Conway in Orange County where 100 settlers, joined later by families and laborers, established homes and citrus groves. Granville Chetwynd Stapylton acquired land north of Leesburg near present-day Fruitland Park in Lake County and established an agricultural training school at the Chetwynd community for young British men. Arthur Fell and partners acquired 12,000 acres east of St. Cloud. Fell's younger brother, E. Nelson Fell, became resident manager at a town he named Narcoossee, surrounded by small homesteads and citrus groves. By 1888, more than 200 British settlers were at Narcoossee. Other communities of British settlers followed.

At each of the 1880s British communities, the immigrants established the social and religious organizations and the recreational activities they had experienced in Britain. English social clubs, dance halls, theatres, tennis courts, yacht clubs, cricket fields and polo grounds became fixtures. The immigrants participated in horse races, fox hunts, and regattas. Some of their churches can be visited today.

The enticing *Times* of London real estate ads of the early 1880s had not included warnings of possible freezing weather during winter months in Florida. Although such freezes were rare in central Florida, brutally cold temperatures in the high teens and low twenties swept through Florida in 1894 and 1895 as far south as Manatee River. Two winters of back-to-back freezes killed the citrus trees at the groves in central Florida. Most of the English homesteads were abandoned, half of the settlers returned to England, and those who stayed moved to Orlando and nearby towns.

Lawn tennis club at Narcoossee, 1890s.
(Image courtesy of the State Archives of Florida)

CENTRAL REGION

where they held regattas. The Polo Club was conceived originally by retired army officer General J.S. Swindler who arrived in 1886 and bought a large grove and acreage west of Orlando. Game play was started in 1888 with the team playing at a field in Conway, now covered by the Dover Shores Shopping Center. In 1890, the Englishmen organized the 100-member Orlando Polo Club, bringing teams from other states to play on a field in Conway. Florida cow ponies were used in the games. In Orlando, they built the Rogers Building where they established the English Club House that was devoted to indoor games. Dudley G. Cary-Elwes, a retired army officer, built a home on Lake Fredericka in 1886 and was instrumental in holding the colony together and in building the Protestant Episcopal Church. After the devastating 1894-1895 freezes that killed most of the orange groves in Orange County, approximately 200 Englishmen abandoned their homes and returned to England or made new homes in Australia, New Zealand, and South Africa."

Orlando

BUMBY BUILDING
102-110 West Church Street

Among the earliest immigrants to arrive with the influx of British settlers to Central Florida during the late 19th century was Joseph Bumby, Sr. who came from England in 1873 and acquired 160 acres for citrus production near present-day Orlando. While waiting for the trees to mature, Bumby became involved in a series of business enterprises including carrying mail between Orlando and Mellonville, operating a stagecoach and freight line between Orlando and Sanford, and establishing an agricultural supply business. When the South Florida Railroad arrived in Orlando in 1880, he became the city's first passenger and freight agent. In 1886, he constructed a building for his new hardware business, one of the earliest brick structures in Orlando. The Bumby Hardware Store continued in family operation at this location until 1966 when the store was closed. The Bumby Building is now in use as part of the Church Street Station dining and entertainment complex.

ROGERS BUILDING
37 South Magnolia Avenue

Known locally as the English Club, the Rogers Building was constructed in 1886 by Gordon Rogers in the Queen Anne style. Born in England, Rogers came to Florida in 1883 with the wave of British settlers who emigrated to Central Florida in the late 19th century to establish citrus groves. After trying for three years to cultivate oranges in Marion County, he relocated to Orlando where he erected the building which bears his name and established a major wholesale company and retail grocery in its first floor. Reportedly, the pressed metal siding, which is very rare in Florida, was shipped from England. The building's second story was occupied shortly after its construction through at least the first decade of the 20th century by the English Club, a social organization formed in 1886 by English immigrants to Orlando and the surrounding area. The Club sponsored a variety of social events and activities for the large English community, including dances, theatrical productions, card playing, and billiards. In subsequent years, the building housed newspaper offices, dance studios, a hotel, restaurants, and other business ventures. Today, the Rogers Building is in use primarily as an art gallery.

OSCEOLA COUNTY
Narcoossee

NARCOOSSEE SCHOOLHOUSE
North Narcoossee Road and Yukon Street
narcoosseehistory.org

In 1883, a company headed by British entrepreneur Arthur Fell purchased 12,000 acres in present-day Osceola County. Two thousand acres were set aside for the townsite of Narcoossee while the remainder was sold as small farmsteads and orange groves. Among those put in charge of the enterprise was Fell's younger brother E. Nelson Fell. The new community

Narcoossee Schoolhouse, Osceola County.
(Image courtesy of the Narcoossee Area Chapter of the Osceola County Historical Society)

CENTRAL REGION

was promoted in England as a great economic opportunity and, by 1888, more than 200 British immigrants had settled in Narcoossee. Following the Great Freezes of 1894-1895 and 1899 which devastated the region's agricultural industry, Narcoossee's population quickly dwindled. E. Nelson Fell eventually settled in Indian River County in 1911 where he established the town of Fellsmere. Among the few buildings left from the English settlement is the Narcoossee Schoolhouse, constructed in ca. 1886. The schoolhouse was also used as a church for the settlement prior to the construction of a church building and, in later years, for chamber of commerce and volunteer firefighter activities. The building is in the process of being restored for use as a local history museum by the Narcoossee Area Chapter of the Osceola County Historical Society.

St. Cloud

FORMER CHURCH OF ST. LUKE AND ST. PETER
813 10th Street

This former church building was originally located in the community of Narcoossee, established by British settlers in the late 19th century. Construction of a church for the community was begun in 1892. Named the St. Peter's Episcopal Church, it was completed in 1898. Beginning in 1930, the church at Narcoossee was dismantled piece by piece with each piece marked and reassembled on Florida Avenue in nearby St. Cloud. The first service in the renamed Church of St. Luke and St. Peter was held in 1931. The building was moved again in 1970 to its current location on 10th Street. In 1990, the congregation moved to another location in the city and the church structure has served as a wedding chapel and then as a preschool and child care facility.

Former church of St. Luke and St. Peter at its original location in Narcoossee.
(Image courtesy of the Narcoossee Area Chapter of the Osceola County Historical Society)

POLK COUNTY

Lakeland

"ACTON COMMUNITY" STATE HISTORICAL MARKER
East Memorial Boulevard and Interlachen Parkway

The text of this marker reads: "In 1884, a group of Englishmen established Acton, named after English author Lord Acton, two miles east of Lakeland. Acton lasted from 1884 until 1894 when its residents scattered after the great freeze. During its decade of existence the town had about 200 people, a hotel, sawmill, stores and a church. Its atmosphere, dress and custom were typically English. Polo, fox hunting and cricket were a part of the village's daily life."

State Historical Marker for the Acton Community.
(Image courtesy of Vale Fillmon, Florida State Historical Marker Program)

CENTRAL REGION

"LODWICK SCHOOL OF AERONAUTICS" HISTORICAL MARKER
2301 Lakeland Hills Boulevard

In 1940, Albert Lodwick moved his civilian flight training school from Lincoln, Nebraska to Lakeland where he leased the Municipal Airport as his home base for the school. That same year, the US Army contracted with the school to provide basic flight training to Army Air Force cadets. In 1941, just prior to America's entry into World War II, arrangements were made to begin training British Royal Air Force (RAF) cadets at American training facilities away from German bombing raids on England. The Lodwick School in Lakeland was one of several major facilities in Florida which provided training to RAF cadets for service in World War II. After the war, the airport was closed and the site developed as the Tigertown baseball complex. In 1994, the City of Lakeland erected a historical marker for the Lodwick School adjacent to its Parks and Recreation office at Tigertown which notes that over 1,200 RAF pilots were trained there.

Dr. Andrew Turnbull's Smyrnea Settlement at New Smyrna Beach and Edgewater, 1766-1778

Dr. Andrew Turnbull's Smyrnea Settlement at today's New Smyrna Beach and Edgewater was a gigantic agricultural enterprise worked by indentured laborers and enslaved Africans, that represents one of the most significant and controversial settlements in all of North American colonial history. The 1,403 indentured laborers Dr. Turnbull recruited from Italy, Greece, and Minorca represent the largest importation of Europeans to a single settlement in any European overseas colony. When the approximately 100 enslaved Africans who Turnbull purchased are counted, along with European carpenters, managers, and their families, the Smyrnea population rivaled that of St. Augustine.

At Smyrnea, the laborers cleared brush and forest to cultivate indigo and food crops, dug miles of canals to drain wetlands for fields of sugar cane, built canoes and schooners, and erected stone wharves, sawmills, windmills, and a sizeable town of dwellings, artisan shops, and storage buildings. Cabins and gardens stretched along the Halifax River for nearly eight miles. The great tragedy of Smyrnea is that more than half of the settlers and slaves died during its existence, mostly of disease. Of the millions of dollars (in contemporary money) invested by Turnbull and his partners, Sir William Duncan and Sir George Grenville, all was lost when the laborers accused Turnbull of abusive treatment and abandoned their cabins to resettle in St. Augustine. One year later, in 1778, the Smyrnea Settlement was abandoned.

In the inevitable accusations and lawsuits that followed the settlement's demise, Turnbull was temporarily imprisoned when he was unable to post a security bond. Freed on bond, he immediately moved to Charleston, South Carolina, where he lived out the remainder of his days. The Mediterranean laborers who survived the experience at Smyrnea became an integral part of St. Augustine's population. Their descendants, often referred to collectively as Minorcans, are still an important component of life in the Ancient City.

Dr. Andrew Turnbull.
(Image courtesy of the State Archives of Florida)

VOLUSIA COUNTY

Daytona Beach

"THE OLD KINGS ROAD" HISTORICAL MARKER
West International Speedway Boulevard (U.S. 92) west of White Street

The text of this marker reads: "The Old Kings Road crossed north to south near this site. This road was constructed from 1763-1773 by the English, connecting St. Augustine north to St. Mary's River and south to New Smyrna, Florida. First originated as an Indian trail, and later improved by the Spanish. Subsequently the industrious British improved the road to serve the East Coast plantations. The U.S. Army improved the Old Kings Road after 1827." This marker was erected in 1976 in conjunction with the celebration of the American Revolution Bicentennial.

New Smyrna Beach

DR. ANDREW TURNBULL MONUMENT
210 Sams Avenue

The largest attempt at British colonization in the New World occurred in British East Florida in 1768. The Smyrnea Settlement extended eight miles from north to south, and included all of what is today New Smyrna Beach and the northern portion of Edgewater. In 1766, Andrew Turnbull, a wealthy Scottish-born physician, received a land grant from the British government of 20,000 acres about 75 miles south of St. Augustine. A business partner, Sir William Duncan, was granted an adjacent 20,000 acres, with the combined enterprise to be

CENTRAL REGION

managed by Turnbull. Additional land grants eventually increased the plantation to over 100,000 acres. Although a number of agricultural products would be grown on the plantation, the main cash crop was indigo, a plant used to produce a brilliant blue dye which commanded a high price in Europe. The new settlement was named in honor of Turnbull's wife, a native of Smyrna (today's Izmer) in present-day Turkey. To provide the manpower for the plantation, Turnbull recruited some 1,400 indentured laborers from the Mediterranean area, mostly from the British-controlled island of Minorca, in 1767 and 1768.

The settlement was beset with difficulties from the very beginning due to crop failures, disease, inadequate housing, and poor nutrition. Hundreds of settlers died during the first three years of the settlement. From 1771 to 1773, the situation improved somewhat as agricultural crop yields increased. Numerous coquina structures were built, including houses, plantation support structures, storehouses, wharfs (docks), and coquina-lined canals. However, severe drought in 1773 through 1775 and soil depletion adversely affected the crops and the death rate among the settlers began to climb sharply again beginning in 1774. During this period, Turnbull became engaged in a feud with the new Royal Governor of East Florida, Patrick Tonyn. In 1776, Turnbull returned to London in an attempt to have Tonyn removed as governor and to raise more funds for his colony. During Turnbull's extended absence, the colonists' discontent reached a breaking point and, in 1777, most of them left Smyrnea for St. Augustine. Complaining of abuses by Tonyn and his overseers, the colonists were freed of their indenture contracts by Governor Tonyn. To this day, many of the Minorcans' descendants can be found in St. Augustine. Tonyn returned to Smyrnea in late 1777 to find his settlement in total disarray. He soon abandoned the enterprise and relocated to Charleston, South Carolina.

In 1968, the Volusia County Historical Commission erected a small monument in front of the New Smyrna Beach City Hall in honor of Andrew Turnbull. The monument consists of a coquina boulder with an attached bronze plaque which reads "Dr. Andrew Turnbull Dec. 2, 1720 - March 13, 1792 Founder of the largest colony under British rule ever to come to the New World, the New Smyrna Colony of Florida, 1768 – 1778."

Letter from Smyrnea in 1774 to the Lieutenant Governor of East Florida, asking protection against Creek Indian raids.
(Image courtesy of the Museum of Florida History)

NEW SMYRNA MUSEUM OF HISTORY
120 Sams Avenue
386.478.0052
nsbhistory.org

Located in the restored 1925 Old Post Office Building, this museum contains exhibits depicting the history of New Smyrna Beach and southeast Volusia County from prehistoric times to the present day. One museum gallery contains an extensive exhibit on Andrew Turnbull's New Smyrna Settlement of the British Period which includes video programs, a large three-dimensional map of the settlement, and period artifacts.

OLD FORT PARK
200 Block of Sams Avenue

This city park contain a massive coquina stone foundation known locally as the "Old Fort" but which is most likely the remnant of a Smyrnea Settlement structure constructed during the British Period by Andrew Turnbull. Although there is no historical documentation confirming that this was the residence of Andrew Turnbull as some have speculated, there is documentation indicating

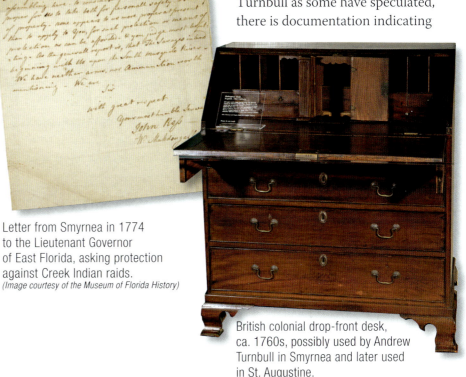

British colonial drop-front desk, ca. 1760s, possibly used by Andrew Turnbull in Smyrnea and later used in St. Augustine.
(Image courtesy of the Museum of Florida History)

Central Region

that Turnbull was building the structure as a home for his partner, Sir William Duncan, who died in 1774 before its completion. In 1998, a bronze plaque for the "1768 British Colony of New Smyrna" was attached to a surrounding park wall by the James Emery Chapter of the National Society Colonial Dames XVII Century. The text of this plaque reads "During Florida's British Colonial Period, 1763-1783, Doctor Andrew Turnbull established the largest North American colony at this site. Approximately 1300 Minorcans, Greeks, and Italians comprised the colony named after Smyrna, Asia Minor, the birthplace of Dr. Turnbull's wife. The colony experienced success in producing indigo dye, rice, hemp, and other crops for shipment to England. Buildings, wharfs, and a canal system, still visible today, were constructed. Despite successes, after nine years, the colony failed. Approximately 600 survivors of the colony relocated to St. Augustine where many descendants reside."

🏛 Old Stone Wharf
South Riverside Drive and Clinch Street

The Old Stone Wharf was constructed by the Turnbull colonists during the British Period as a docking facility for the loading and unloading of sea-going vessels. Most of the wharf is submerged under water, although portions are exposed at low tide. The extant remains of the wharf consist of two coquina block piers on a north-south alignment extending some 90 feet east into the Intracoastal Waterway. A metal marker on a wooden post is located in the water which denotes the "Old Stone Wharf Historic Site Circa 1768." In 1940, a small monument was erected onshore at the wharf site by the Jane Sheldon Chapter of the Daughters of the American

British merchant ship flag, ca. 1900-1925.
(Image courtesy of the Museum of Florida History)

Revolution. The monument consists of an irregular coquina boulder with an attached bronze plaque which reads "Site of Old Stone Wharf built by Turnbull colonists in 1768[.] It formed a terminus of the Kings Road completed in 1771 and marked the beginning point of all of the early surveys of the community. It was the scene of a Civil War engagement March 24, 1862, between the 3rd Florida Regiment and seamen of the Union gunboats 'Henry Andrews' and 'Penguin.'" Although this plaque indicates that the Kings Road terminated here, the road actually continued to the south for another 15 miles to the Elliot Plantation in present-day Brevard County.

Turnbull Canal Monument
North side of intersection of Canal Street and Riverside Drive

As part of Andrew Turnbull's efforts to establish an economic infrastructure for the British Period Smyrnea Settlement, an extensive network of canals was hand-dug by his indentured laborers and lined with coquina rock. The canals were used for draining the low-lying, swampy interior for agriculture and for irrigating crops. In 1968, a bronze plaque was attached by the Jane Sheldon Chapter of the Daughters of the American Revolution to one of two large coquina pillars marking the site of a Smyrnea Settlement canal. The text of the plaque reads: "Turnbull Canal [-] one of two main canals into which flowed the vast network of smaller irrigation and drainage canals from the Turnbull Hammock, through New Smyrna Colony indigo plantations and the farms of Minorcan, Greek, and Italian colonists. Dug during the 1770's by the settlers and [is] still in use today. It was covered in 1924 by the sidewalk on the north side of Canal Street from Myrtle Avenue to Riverside Drive."

Ormond Beach

"Old King's Road" State Historical Marker
Ormond Lakes Boulevard between Emerald Oaks Lane and Lakebluff Drive

The text of this marker reads: "The King's Road (also called Old King's Road- named for King George of

CENTRAL REGION

England) crossed north to south near this site. It was the first graded road built in Florida. Approximately 1.14 miles extends through Ormond Lake's subdivision. Centuries ago, it originated as an Indian trail connecting Timucuan Indian villages along Florida's East Coast. The Spanish laid out the primary trail during their first occupation of Florida (1513-1763). The British developed the winding trail into a working road (1763-1773) as area residents and the British Parliament put up funds for the highway's construction. Among other uses during the British Period (1763-1783), it served the many large plantations being created along Florida's East Coast. During the Second Spanish occupation (1784-1821) the Spanish regained control but preferred water routes to land passages and the King's Road fell into disrepair. Following the American acquisition of Florida in 1821, the United States Congress appropriated funds to reconstruct the road. U.S. Army engineers completed the work between 1828 and 1831. The King's Road was constructed from St. Mary's, Georgia, to New Smyrna Beach, Florida, where it terminates at the remains of a stone wharf."

"OLD KINGS ROAD" HISTORICAL MARKER

North Old King Road and West Granada Boulevard

The text of this marker reads: "The Old Kings Road crossed north to south near this site. First originated as an Indian trail, later improved by the Spanish, and then constructed by the British as a road in 1763-1773 to connect St. Augustine and New Smyrna, Florida. Improved by the United States Army in 1827." This marker was erected in 1976 in conjunction with the celebration of the American Revolution Bicentennial by the Ormond Beach Rotary Club.

The King's Road: Florida's First Highway

Early in his tenure as governor of East Florida, James Grant realized that the few narrow trails existing in the province were fit only for foot or horse traffic under optimal conditions and often impassable in rainy weather. The governor's efforts to persuade settlers to move to Florida were stymied when families traveling by wagon encountered bad roads and a lack of bridges and ferry boats. Lacking construction funds, the governor saved money from the annual provincial budgets and made plans for a road to run north from the southernmost plantation on the Atlantic Coast through St. Augustine and to the border with Georgia at the St. Marys River.

Grant was in London in March 1772 when funding became available for the road. He immediately sent orders to interim-governor John Moultrie to negotiate contracts for a roadway to be built in segments. The road was to measure 16 feet wide, with ditches, pine logs laid crosswise in wet sections (called corduroy ribbing), causeways through swamps, and bridges spanning creeks and rivers. The governor warned that he would one day travel the road in a carriage and he would be furious if he found a "bad stop or an insufficient bridge."

The southern segment of the road extended for 90 miles, passing through London merchant Richard Oswald's 20,000-acre estate at Tomoka River, Dr. Andrew Turnbull's 40,000-acre Smyrnea Plantation at Mosquito Inlet, and terminating at Stobbs Farm, owned by another London merchant, William Elliot. Enslaved black men owned by John Moultrie raised the height of the causeway that led from the western wall of St. Augustine to a new bridge that was constructed across the St. Sebastian River. From there, slaves owned by Richard Payne completed the road to Matanzas River. Robert Bisset, a retired army officer and East Florida planter, supervised as slaves cut trees and stumps low to permit carriage wheels to pass over, dug drainage ditches, and packed the roadways.

Old King's Road historical marker, Daytona Beach.
(Image courtesy of Vale Fillmon, Florida State Historical Marker Program).

Work on the southern portion of the roadway was completed in July 1774, after James Grant resigned as governor and became a Member of Parliament. The Reverend John Forbes wrote to him: "The road really may with propriety be called the King's Highway, it forms a wide beautiful avenue, not a stump of tree to be found."

North of St. Augustine, a 35 mile segment extended to a ferry crossing on the south bank of the St. Johns River known as the Cowford (across from today's downtown center in Jacksonville). Work on this portion of the road was completed in July 1774 by enslaved black men owned by John Fairlamb and Joshua Yallowly, planters who resided near the ferry.

The northernmost segment of the King's Road extended from the north bank of the St. Johns to a ferry landing on the south bank of the St. Marys River, 40 miles from the ocean, at a place known to locals as William Mill's trade store. The contractors for the northern segment were Charles and Jermyn Wright, Florida planters and brothers of the Royal Governor of Georgia, James Wright. Jermyn Wright operated a major rice plantation on the St. Marys.

The King's Road in East Florida was completed in the first half of 1775. Within weeks the American War for Independence was underway and the loyal residents of East Florida had become war-time enemies of the rebels of Georgia. The newly completed King's Road became a convenient travel route for the contending armies and guerrilla bands that ravaged settlements on both sides of the St. Marys River. Later, refugees who remained loyal to the Crown and Parliament followed the route to Loyalist East Florida with their families and slaves, only to experience further heartbreak when the colony was ceded back to Spain in 1783.

CENTRAL REGION

TOMOKA STATE PARK
2099 North Beach Street
386.676.4050
floridastateparks.org/tomoka

During the British Period, a portion of the 20,000-acre Mount Oswald Plantation was located in the present-day Tomoka State Park. The plantation was owned by the Scottish-born Richard Oswald, a wealthy London maritime merchant, ship owner, and slave trader. Oswald never visited Florida himself, but rather operated his plantation through overseers who managed the property with slave labor on his behalf. Development of the Mount Oswald Plantation began in 1766 and, in little more than a decade, an expansive plantation complex of five separate settlements had been created. This vast agricultural enterprise included extensive indigo fields with processing facilities, rice fields with dikes, canals and dams, sugar cane fields with sugar processing buildings and a rum distillery, cotton fields, and a cattle ranch. Despite enormous environmental obstacles, Mount Oswald Plantation was poised to become a highly profitable estate. However, its development was disrupted, and then finally ended, by events related to the American Revolution. Following a Spanish raid on English plantations in the Mosquito Inlet area in 1780, Mount Oswald Plantation temporarily ceased operations. In 1782, Oswald was selected by the British government to negotiate preliminary peace terms with the Americans which led to the 1783 Treaty of Paris ending the American Revolution. With the return of Florida to the Spanish under treaty terms, Oswald ordered Mt. Oswald Plantation abandoned in 1784.

A small monument for the "Mount Oswald Plantation" was erected in Tomoka State Park by the Volusia County Historical Commission in 1975. The monument consists of a coquina boulder with an attached metal plaque which reads "In 1766 Richard Oswald acquired 20,000 acres of land along the Halifax and Tomoka rivers from the British government. On this grant was established Mount Oswald Plantation which was located on this site, and produced indigo, rice, timber, molasses, rum, sugar and oranges. In 1785, after the British exodus from Florida, Mount Oswald was abandoned. Oswald's major contribution to history was his participation in the preliminary peace negotiations at the end of the American Revolution. He was a signer of the preliminary peace treaty for the British, and his American counterparts were Benjamin Franklin, John Jay, John Adams and Henry Laurens. Oswald has been given the credit and the blame for negotiating a peace so favorable to the United States."

Mount Oswald Plantation monument, Tomoka State Park.
(Image courtesy of Vale Fillmon, Florida State Historical Marker Program)

THREE CHIMNEYS
715 West Granada Boulevard
386.677.7005
ormondhistory.org/3Chimneys.htm

The Three Chimneys site contains the remains of what is believed to be the oldest extant sugar mill and rum distillery in Florida. Established during the British Period, this site was one of five settlements created within the 20,000-acre Mount Oswald Plantation estate owned by Richard Oswald. Known as Swamp Settlement, it consisted of some 300 cleared acres for growing sugarcane and several structures for processing the sugarcane to sugar and producing rum. Buildings included a grinding mill, boiler, warehouses, and distillery. Enslaved Africans provided the labor under the direction of a Jamaican planter sent by Oswald. It may have been in operation as early as 1770. At the end of the British Period, the settlement was abandoned along with the rest of Mount Oswald Plantation. The site subsequently became known as Three Chimneys, although it is not understood where this name came from as there is only above-ground evidence for two. The current remaining site of approximately eight acres contains the ruins of the sugarcane juice boiling facility and the rum distillery. The boiler consisted of a long structure of handmade red brick with four kettles and four separate fireboxes, or furnaces, for fueling the boiling process. The distillery, made of handmade red brick on a coquina foundation, had two fireboxes on either side of a chimney which collapsed in 1997. In 2003, the site was purchased by the State of Florida and then leased to the Ormond Beach Historical Society for management and public interpretation. A State Historical Marker at the site, and another erected by the National Society of the Daughters of the American Colonists, provide information on its history.

South Region

DeSoto County
Arcadia

British Royal Air Force Training Fields
Carlstrom Field, 5847 SE Highway 31 and Dorr Field, 13617 SE Highway 70

In 1917, Carlstrom Field and a satellite airfield at Dorr Field were established near Arcadia to train pilots for service in World War I. Both fields were closed in the post-war period but reopened in 1941 under contract with the Riddle Aeronautical Institute to provide primary flight training for both American Army Air Force and British Royal Air Force cadets. Over 1,300 British RAF pilot trainees received instruction at the facilities for service in World War II. Two of the RAF cadets died from non-flying related causes at Carlstrom Field and are buried in Arcadia's Oak Ridge Cemetery. Both airfields were closed after the war. Carlstrom Field became the site of the G. Pierce Wood Memorial Hospital in 1947 until its closing in 2002. It then became the DeSoto Juvenile Correctional Facility until it was closed in 2011. Dorr Field was converted for use as the DeSoto Correctional Institution. World War II-era buildings remained in use at both facilities in their new roles.

Cemetery plot for British Royal Air Force cadets at Oak Ridge Cemetery, Arcadia.
(Image courtesy of the State Archives of Florida)

British RAF cadets in training at Carlstrom Field near Arcadia.
(Image courtesy of the British Imperial War Museums)

Oak Ridge Cemetery
Oak Ridge Street

With burials dating to the late 19th century, the historic Oak Ridge Cemetery in northwest Arcadia is perhaps best known for an event that occurs there each Memorial Day. During World War II, 23 British Royal Air Force cadets who died during flight training were buried in this cemetery. Two died at Carlstrom Field at Arcadia while the other 21 died at Riddle Field at nearby Clewiston. Nineteen died in training flight crashes, two from illness, one in an automobile accident, and one from drowning. These RAF cadets are buried in a specially designated area of the cemetery surrounded by a low masonry wall which contains granite headstones and a flagpole that flies the British Union Jack flag. The entry threshold is engraved with "Commonwealth War Graves." Nearby is a short upright granite monument containing a bronze plaque with a short history of the RAF training in the area and the care of the cadets' graves. In 1968, the Rotary Club of Arcadia erected a commemorative marker in the cemetery for "The British Plot." In 1989, a headstone for the RAF cadets' American civilian instructor, John Paul Riddle, was erected in the plot after his ashes were scattered over the Atlantic Ocean. Starting in 1956 and conducted every subsequent year, the Arcadia Rotary Club sponsors a service on Memorial Day in honor of the RAF cadets. British officials routinely attend the ceremony which features the playing of bagpipes, the singing of "God Save The Queen," and a special flyover by a propeller plane.

 # South Region

British Wings Over Florida in World War II

After hearing British Prime Minister Winston Churchill's February 1941 speech requesting aid for his nation's war against Germany, U.S. President Franklin Delano Roosevelt and the United States Congress agreed to the Lend-Lease Act. Over the next five years, American factories produced military products for the Allied nations, with the expectation that repayment would come after the war ended. Also implemented in 1941 was a program authorizing American instructors to train British pilots at British Flying Training (BFT) Schools established in the United States at Texas, California, Oklahoma, Arizona, and Florida. The BFT School No. 5 was located in Florida at Riddle Field near Clewiston.

Royal Air Force cadets also received flight training at Carlstrom and Dorr Fields near Arcadia, the Lodwick School of Aeronautics at Lakeland, and at Naval Air Station Pensacola. The cadets at the flight training schools were housed in barracks and fed at mess halls on their respective bases. At the Pan American Airways facility in Coral Gables, Royal Air Force cadets studied navigation and meteorology and were housed and fed at the University of Miami.

Thousands of young British men were trained as pilots and navigators in Florida during World War II. They were generally transported to Canada by ship and from there were sent to bases in the state by train. In Florida, skies were generally clear, at least in comparison to the often cloudy and rainy conditions in Britain, and cadets and instructors could train without the threat of being shot down by German planes. They were also welcome guests in the homes of residents of the nearby towns, and for some, lifelong friendships were forged.

British RAF cadets and their instructor at Carlstrom Field near Arcadia.
(Image courtesy of the State Archives of Florida)

Royal Air Force (RAF) cloth pilot's wings of a British aviator who trained at Arcadia in WWII.
(Image courtesy of the family of RAF pilot Clifford G. R. Coffee)

HENDRY COUNTY
Clewiston

British Royal Air Force Memorial
Civic Park
100 Block of West Sugarland Highway

In 1941, Riddle Field was constructed west of Clewiston to provide flight training by the Riddle-McKay Aero College to British Royal Air Force and American pilots. Designated as the No. 5 British Flying Training School (BFTS), over 1,300 British cadets learned to fly at the facility during World War II. Twenty-one of the RAF cadets died while in training at Riddle Field, mostly from flying-related accidents, and are buried at the Oak Ridge Cemetery in nearby Arcadia. After the war, Riddle Field was eventually acquired by Hendry County and Airglades Airport was constructed at the site. The wartime buildings were demolished and replaced by modern ones, but a British Union Jack flag flies at the airport in honor of the BFTS. In memory of the RAF cadets who trained at Clewiston, a memorial was erected in the city's downtown central park. The masonry monument contains two plaques, the largest of which honors the "No. 5 British Flying Training School" with a smaller one above it providing a history of "Riddle Field, Clewiston."

Clewiston Museum
109 Central Avenue
863.983.2870
clewistonmuseum.org

Located in the 1928 Old Clewiston News Building, the Clewiston Museum contains exhibits which tell the story of the community's history from prehistoric times to the present. The museum contains an exhibit on the "Number 5 British Flying Training School," which was located at nearby Riddle Field during World War II, with related artifacts and historic photographs.

SOUTH REGION

MIAMI-DADE COUNTY
Homestead

**BISCAYNE NATIONAL PARK
DANTE FASCELL
VISITOR CENTER**
Convoy Point
9700 SW 328th Street
305.230.7275
nps.gov/bisc

In 1975, the remains of a shipwreck, subsequently identified as the 18th century British warship HMS *Fowey*, were located by National Park Service (NPS) underwater archaeologists at what is known today as the Legare Anchorage in Biscayne National Park off the coast of southeast Florida. Launched in 1744 at Hull, England, the HMS *Fowey* was originally armed with 20 cannons and contained a crew of over 200 men, and was rearmed in 1745 with 44 cannons. The vessel saw service in European, Caribbean and North American waters during which time she captured a French ship during convoy duty from Jamaica to England and sank another in an engagement off the coast of France. In 1748, the HMS *Fowey* sank after hitting a reef near Elliott Key while escorting a Spanish merchant ship she had captured and two British colonial merchant vessels. In 1978, a sport diver filed a court claim to obtain rights to salvage the remains of the ship, but litigation in federal courts affirmed that the shipwreck was public property in a National Park. Subsequent NPS excavations of the shipwreck site identified it as the HMS *Fowey* and numerous artifacts, including cannons, from the ship were recovered. A number of these artifacts are on display in an exhibit at the Biscayne National Park's Visitor Center museum.

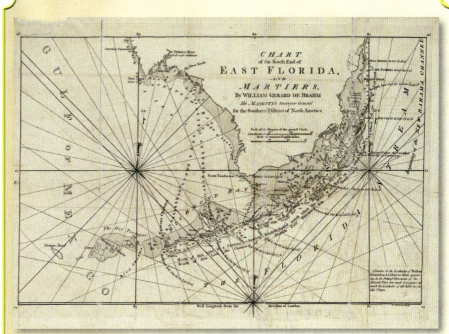

Map of southeast Florida by John William Gerard de Brahm, 1772.
(Image courtesy of the Norman B. Leventhal Map Center, Boston Public Library)

Frederick Mulcaster and the Exploration of Southeast Florida

In 1772, the Surveyor General of East Florida, Frederick Mulcaster, wrote the classic description of an undeveloped and largely uninhabited southeast Florida. Mulcaster is believed to have been a half-brother of King George III. Both men were apparently fathered by Frederick, Prince of Wales, although born to different mothers; Mulcaster out of wedlock. A graduate of the Royal Military Academy at Woolwich, Mulcaster eventually achieved the rank of major-general in the British army.

In February 1772, Mulcaster traveled from St. Augustine to today's Dade County to survey tracts along Biscayne Bay for absentee British landowners. Traveling with several men in two sailing vessels, one a schooner large enough to carry two horses and a heavy load of measuring chains, axes, cooking utensils, provisions, and tools for wilderness survival, Mulcaster arrived at Biscayne Bay on March 13. It had been a difficult journey, and Mulcaster had been forced to leave his horses at today's St. Lucie Inlet.

For the next four weeks, he explored the shores of Biscayne Bay surveying tracts in today's Dade and Broward counties and found the region entirely devoid of human inhabitants. At Biscayne Bay, they found "a channel of above a quarter of a mile wide with above 13 ft. of water without a breaker and the water so clear that you might see to pick a sixpence at the bottom. The main land...consists of large fresh marshes, and rich open savannahs..." heavily timbered with a wide variety of trees. After exploring four small rivers that emptied into the head of the bay, Mulcaster concluded that "no man has been up [the rivers] for fifty or sixty years" although he did find that "upon some of these rivers may be seen the remains of old Indian fields."

After surveying several 20,000 acre tracts, Mulcaster ended his enterprise and started back to St. Augustine. It was a harrowing and life-threatening journey. Mulcaster wrote that he survived "the last five weeks on the chance of powder and ball, no bread, rice, flour, or biscuit" until he reached the southernmost British plantation, Stobbs Farm (today near Oak Hill) owned by London merchant William Elliot, in late April. Mulcaster was relieved to find himself "in perfect health."

South Region

Miami Beach

Deauville Beach Resort
6701 Collins Avenue
305.865.8511
deauvillebeachresort.com

Designed by noted architect Melvin Grossman, the Deauville Hotel (now the Deauville Beach Resort) opened in 1958. In 1964, the hotel became the scene of a musical "British invasion" when it was the site of the Beatles' second televised appearance in the United States. The Beatles made their memorable American debut on the *Ed Sullivan Show* in the CBS television studio in New York City on February 9, 1964. Following concerts in Washington, D.C. and Carnegie Hall in New York City, the Beatles flew to Florida where they made their second live televised appearance on the *Ed Sullivan Show* from the Napoleon Ballroom of the Deauville Hotel on February 16, 1964. The performance was attended by about 3,500 people but viewed by an estimated 70 million people via satellite broadcast. The Beatles remained at the Deauville Hotel while they participated in a number of photo sessions in the area including one with Cassius Clay, later known as Muhammad Ali, at a Miami gym before departing to England on February 21, 1964. The Beatles returned to Florida later that year as part of a month-long concert tour of the United States and Canada. Their scheduled flight from Montreal, Canada to Jacksonville on September 9, 1964 was diverted to Key West due to Hurricane Dora which would strike northeast Florida the next day. After spending two days in Key West at the Key Wester Motel (demolished in 1999), the Beatles performed a concert at the Gator Bowl in Jacksonville on September 11, 1964. It would be their last concert in Florida as a group.

Miami

Woodlawn Park Cemetery
3260 SW 8th Street

Established in 1913, the Woodlawn Park Cemetery contains a special section with thirteen British Commonwealth war dead from World War II. Within this well-kept plot are the graves of eleven British aviators, one from the Royal Air Force and ten from the Royal Navy, as well as two aviators from the Royal New Zealand Navy. These men died while in training at the Naval Air Station Miami which consisted of three separate airfields: Opa-locka or Mainside, Miami Municipal, and Master Field.

Monroe County

Key West

Mel Fisher Maritime Museum
200 Greene Street
305.294.2633
melfisher.org

Artifacts from the British slave ship *Henrietta Marie* are displayed in a major permanent exhibit at the Mel Fisher Maritime Museum. Probably built in France, the ship came into English possession late in the 17th century, possibly as a war prize. It wasantic slave trade, transporting enslaved Africans to the West Indies. In May 1700, the *Henrietta Marie* delivered some 200 slaves to Jamaica but, on its return voyage to England, wrecked on a reef west of Key West. Its entire crew of about 18 men perished at sea. In 1972, treasure hunters affiliated with Mel Fisher's Treasure Salvors Inc. located the remains of a vessel which became known as the "English Wreck" based on the artifacts collected from it. Excavations in the 1980s identified the vessel as the *Henrietta Marie*. Thousands of artifacts were recovered which were subsequently donated by Mel Fisher to the not-for-profit Mel Fisher Maritime Heritage Society. Collectively, these artifacts represent the largest assemblage of items recovered from a slave ship to date. They include slave shackles, cannons, Venetian glass trade beads, African ivory, and English-made pewter tankards, basins, spoons and bottles. In 1993, the National Association of Black Scuba Divers placed a memorial at the shipwreck site, consisting of a bronze plaque embedded on a three-foot tall concrete block, to the "enslaved African people" carried by the *Henrietta Marie*.

The Beatles in Key West, September 1964.
(Image courtesy of the State Archives of Florida)

Cannon from the "Storm Wreck," a British ship that wrecked off St. Augustine in 1782.
(Image courtesy of the St. Augustine Lighthouse and Museum)

Recovery of the "Storm Wreck" cannon in 2011 by archaeologists of the St. Augustine Lighthouse Archaeological Maritime Program.
(Image courtesy of the St. Augustine Lighthouse and Museum)

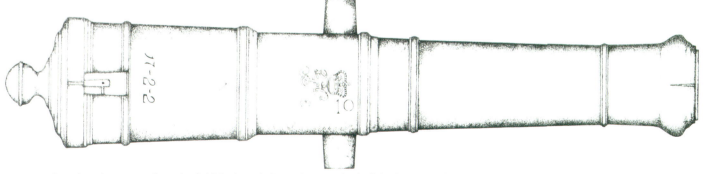
Drawing of a cannon from the British sloop *Industry* that wrecked off St. Augustine in 1764.
(Image courtesy of the St. Augustine Lighthouse and Museum)

Selected Bibliography

Printed Resources:

Bailyn, Bernard. "Failure in Xanadu," and "Gulf and Delta," in *Voyagers to the West: A Passage in the Peopling of America on the Eve of the Revolution.* New York: Alfred A. Knopf, 1985.

Cashin, Edward J. *The King's Ranger: Thomas Brown and the American Revolution on the Southern Frontier.* Athens: The University of Georgia Press, 1989.

Covington, James W. *The British Meet the Seminoles: Negotiations Between British Authorities in East Florida and the Indians: 1763-68.* Gainesville: University of Florida Press, 1961.

De Quesada, Alejandro M. *Images of America: The Royal Air Force Over Florida.* Charleston, SC: Arcadia Publishing, 1998.

Fabel, Robin F.A. *Bombast and Broadsides: The Lives of George Johnstone.* Tuscaloosa: University of Alabama Press, 1987.

_____. *The Economy of British West Florida, 1763-1783.* Tuscaloosa: University of Alabama Press, 1988.

Forbes, James Grant. *Sketches, Historical and Topographical, of the Floridas; more particularly of East Florida.* New York: C.S. Van Winkle, 1831.

Gordon, Elsbeth. *Florida's Colonial Architectural Heritage.* Gainesville: University Press of Florida, 2002.

Griffin, Patricia C. *Mullet on the Beach: The Minorcans of Florida, 1768-1788.* Jacksonville: University of North Florida Press, 1991.

Harper, Francis, ed. "Diary of a Journey through the Carolinas, Georgia, and Florida from July 1, 1765 to April 10, 1766". *Transactions of The American Philosophical Society* 33, No. 1, Philadelphia, 1942.

_____. *The Travels of William Bartram: Naturalist Edition.* Athens: University of Georgia Press: 1998.

Hoffman, Paul E. *Florida's Frontiers.* Bloomington: Indiana University Press, 2002.

Landers, Jane G. ed. *Colonial Plantations and Economy in Florida.* Gainesville: University Press of Florida, 2000.

Largent, Will. *RAF Wings Over Florida.* West Lafayette, IN: Purdue University Press, 2000.

Mowat, Charles. *East Florida as a British Province, 1763-1784.* 1943, facsimile reprint: Gainesville: University of Florida Press, 1964.

Nelson, Paul David. *General James Grant: Scottish Soldier and Royal Governor of East Florida.* Gainesville: University Press of Florida, 1993.

Panagopoulos, Epaminondas P. *New Smyrna: An Eighteenth-Century Greek Colony.* Gainesville: University of Florida Press, 1966.

Patterson, Gordon. "Ditches and Dreams, Nelson Fell and the Rise of Fellsmere." *The Florida Historical Quarterly.* Vol. 76, No. 1 (Summer 1997), 1-19.

Rea, Robert R. "Pensacola under the British (1763-1781)." In *Colonial Pensacola*, James R. McGovern, ed. Hattiesburg: University of Southern Mississippi Press, 1972.

Schafer, Daniel L. *Governor James Grant's Villa: A British East Florida Indigo Plantation.* St. Augustine Historical Society, 2000.

_____. *St. Augustine's British Years, 1763-1784.* St. Augustine Historical Society, 2001.

_____. *William Bartram and the Ghost Plantations of British East Florida.* Gainesville: University Press of Florida, 2010.

Searcy, Martha Condray. *The Georgia-Florida Contest in the American Revolution, 1776-1778.* Tuscaloosa: University of Alabama Press, 1985.

Starr, Joseph Barton. *Tories, Dons, and Rebels: The American Revolution in West Florida.* Gainesville: University Presses of Florida, 1976.

Troxler, Carole Watterson. "Loyalist Refugees and the Evacuation of East Florida, 1783-1785." *The Florida Historical Quarterly.* Vol. 60, No. 1 (July 1981), 1-28.

Weisman, Brent R. *Unconquered Peoples: Florida's Seminole and Miccosukee Indians.* Gainesville: University Press of Florida, 1999.

Wright, J. Leitch, Jr. *Britain and the American Frontier, 1783-1815.* Athens: The University of Georgia Press, 1975.

_____. *Florida in the American Revolution.* Gainesville: University Presses of Florida, 1975.

Internet Web Site:

"New World in a State of Nature: British East Florida." *Florida History Online.* Daniel L. Schafer, Department of History, University of North Florida
unf.edu/floridahistoryonline

ACKNOWLEDGEMENTS

**Artifact Photography
(Museum of Florida History)**
Ray Stanyard

Biscayne National Park
Charles Lawson

City of Orlando
Richard Forbes

Florida Association of Museums
Malinda Horton

**Florida Division
of Historical Resources**
Vale Fillmon
Christopher Fowler
Grant Gelhardt
Kechia Herring
Susanne Hunt

**Florida Public
Archaeology Network**
Dr. William Lees

Mandarin Museum
Bruce Vacca

Museum of Florida History
Bruce Graetz
Kieran O. Holland

Museum of Science and History
Christy Leonard

**Orange County
Regional History Center**
Sara Van Arsdel

**Osceola County Historical Society
Narcoossee Area Chapter**
Lisa Liu

Pena-Peck House
Margo Pope

Putnam County Bartram Trail
Sam Carr

State Archives of Florida
N. Adam Watson

St. Augustine Historical Society
Charles Tingley

**St. Augustine
Lighthouse & Museum**
Kathy Fleming
Chuck Meide
Shannon O'Neil

St. Johns County
Robin Moore

View of Pensacola during the British Period, 1770s.
(Image courtesy of the Library of Congress)

"The Taking of Pensacola" depicting the Spanish capture in May 1781 of the British Queen's Redoubt at the Battle of Pensacola during the American Revolution.
(Artist: Hugh Charles McBarron, Jr., Image courtesy of the U.S. Army Center of Military History)